From the Heart

*Men and Women Write Their Private Thoughts
About Their Married Lives*

EDITED BY
DALE ATKINS, PH.D., & MERIS POWELL, M.A.

Henry Holt and Company ❧ New York

Henry Holt and Company, Inc.
Publishers since 1866
115 West 18th Street
New York, New York 10011

Henry Holt® is a registered trademark
of Henry Holt and Company, Inc.

Published in Canada by Fitzhenry & Whiteside Ltd.,
195 Allstate Parkway, Markham, Ontario L3R 4T8.

Library of Congress Cataloging-in-Publication Data
Atkins, Dale V. and Powell, Meris.
From the Heart.
From the heart: men and women write their private thoughts
about their married lives / edited by Dale V. Atkins,
and Meris Powell.—1st ed.
p.   cm
1. Married people—Correspondence.   2. Marriage.
I. Atkins, Dale V.   II. Powell, Meris.
HQ734.F777   1995   94-22152
306.81—dc20   CIP

ISBN 0-8050-3498-6

Henry Holt books are available for special promotions
and premiums. For details contact: Director, Special Markets.

First Edition—1994

Designed by Betty Lew

Printed in the United States of America
All first editions are printed on acid-free paper.∞

1   3   5   7   9   10   8   6   4   2

To our extraordinary children,
Jonathan and Joshua Rosen and Katherine Prescott,
and our parents, Sylvia and Jerry Atkins
and Nina and Harold Menowitz.

And to our remarkable husbands,
Rob Rosen and Darrell Prescott, with whom
we are discovering life, love, and marriage.

Contents

Preface   xiii

"It seemed to me he was protecting his heart"   1

"My sex drive isn't at its height on a usual weeknight"   2

"We are both equally convinced we are right"   5

"Marriage is an intensely personal journey"   7

"She reminded me of what's truly important"   10

"If I had to do it over again, I would do it
    over again"   12

"The opposition we faced was the greatest
    wedding gift"   15

"I can no longer tell where he ends and
    where I begin"   19

"Marriage isn't an entitlement to change a person"   24

"Since then we've changed our lives again"   27

"Andre helped take away the loneliness"   30

"Memories are all we truly own"   31

"We were on automatic"   34

"I'm still very much in love with my wife"   35

"We choose partners for many reasons"   38

"I was angry at myself for having pushed her so far"   42

"Marriage falls easily into dangerous tedium"   44

"Our marriage continues to demand the best from us"   47

"I wanted so much from my marriage"   49

"Being a stepmother has enriched my life"   53

"Our love has many faces"   57

"The example we set for our children is their legacy"   61

"You Have to Work on It"   65

"He was fighting for his life"   67

"We were trapped together, and we could
   escape together"   71

"Take a risk, break some rules"   72

"The minute you become involved, your life changes"   73

"After twenty-eight years, we're comfortable"   78

"Thank you for staying with me"   81

"We choose each other every day in small ways"   85

"Remember that passion is not love"   88

"What has kept us together are the qualities we share" 90

"I am so proud you are my Wifey" 92

"All any of us really wants is to feel understood" 93

"I've learned a new technique: hostility
  management" 98

"A common study is a great bonding force" 103

"Why don't more couples work together?" 106

"We made the right decision at the outset" 108

"Marriage would be easier if one had a guidebook" 111

"Ken would have taken care of his Barbie" 112

"I had a great need for others to approve
  of my husband" 116

"My children think I'm lonely, but I'm not" 118

"I was determined never to become a bitchy wife" 120

"All of us nurtured by the marriage grow" 122

"I have more to learn from my parents' relationship" 124

"There are certain things we will never say" 126

"The essence of marriage is the ability to
  share power" 130

"I didn't know if there would be enough love
  and time" 134

"Together we make empty streets interesting" 136

"We still like to be together and laugh" 138

"The stresses tore us apart, then cemented
  us together"   140

"We weathered twenty-eight years of illness"   144

"Who can give us back our joy? Our children"   147

"I am thinking of a kind of wanton happiness"   149

"Marriage does not mean the loss of autonomy"   156

"There are certain requisites for a good,
  happy marriage"   157

"We were dedicated to each other's ideals and truths" 162

"It was his duty to make sure she earned her degree"   166

"We needed to talk and reach agreements
  about our kids"   168

"Our child has become the reason for our marriage" 170

"The sign for stepmother is 'fake mother'"   172

"My tongue has bite marks on it"   173

"I gave him my decision: smoking for gambling"   175

"Money became a wedge between us"   177

"I have him back again"   179

"If you never received love, how can you give it?" 182

"A happy marriage requires a lot of hard work"   186

"There is a contentment now"   189

"There is an abyss dividing us"   192

"You lift my spirits every time I see you"   194

"We won't have the time, so we must make
  the time"   196

"I wish we had more time to just be together"   200

"We don't have sex often"   204

"Our passion gives us a privateness
  in our relationship"   206

"We were like total strangers, still awkward"   208

"The table looks great. The kitchen is a
  disaster zone"   210

"We both must be right at all times"   212

"As we get older we cocoon even more"   214

"I am able to give in and let go of being right"   215

"I would not change a thing"   218

"Your mother never washed her own back"   220

"We try never to go to sleep angry"   222

"We hug each other often"   223

"The shell that made me impervious became porous"   224

"Here we are, wrinkles, bellies, and all, laughing
  more than ever"   229

Afterword   235

Acknowledgments   237

About the Editors   239

*P*reface

When we told people we were working on a book about marriage, the first question they asked, sometimes nervously, was, "Which side are you on?" As if one could find an answer to that question through logic. Yet, without hesitation, but with some clarification, we are "pro." Every marriage differs from all others, not all marriages can be made to work, and there is no ideal relationship. It is up to wives and husbands to agree on what works best for them. *From the Heart* begins here.

We were looking for a way to write about marriage, a way for readers to see how marriages differ from couple to couple and generation to generation, from the viewpoints of men and women. We wanted to give readers direct access to original ideas, unfiltered and unaffected by our biases, or by academic jargon, so they could find their own truths as they do when reading fiction or watching movies.

We decided that letters written by married people about an aspect of their married lives would offer the ideal material for *From the Heart*. We then invited friends, acquaintances, and people we met through our work and our affiliations to write about some aspect of their own married experiences, or an issue they had or had not resolved in their marriages, and we promised them anonymity. We asked them to focus on one topic and provide examples from their own marriages. We urged them to write from their hearts. For a year and a half, we sent letters requesting participation, occasionally adjusting the explanation of what we were looking for, broadening the range of suggested topics, to make sure key issues would be sufficiently discussed from various points of view. We then paired every letter we received with another letter, or letters, to highlight a theme or emotion given voice by its author. The result is a dialogue of sorts, which we as readers are privy to, between letters addressing similar topics.

The contributors are from several countries. Their responsibilities and conflicts, goals and challenges are the same as those faced by most spouses, as are the accommodations they make, with themselves and within their marriages. Most contributors are currently married, many are divorced and remarried. Several are divorced and single. A few are widowed. The longest marriage is sixty-three years, the most recent six months.

Those who participated did so because they were intrigued by the opportunity to participate in a new kind of marriage book, one written by other married people. *From the Heart* is a collection, not a study. It is an "about" book, not a "how-to" book. Many of the letters read like short stories, stories about the complex ties of marriage and the mundane realities of married life. Like autobiographies, they are valuable sources of information about how others lead their lives.

When we met each other, we were in graduate school and we were single. Now we are both married and have children. Being married has not only changed our lives for the better, it has changed us as individuals. Our relationships challenge us in many of the ways the contributors describe. Reading the letters has helped us put our marriages, and our lives, in perspective.

Along the way, we have come to believe that marriages might benefit if husbands and wives were not so quick to conclude, "My marriage doesn't work; how can I get out of it?" and instead posed a different question: "My way of being married isn't working; how else could I be married?"

The letters that follow are about the many ways people are married.

"It seemed to me he was protecting his heart"

Dear Reader,

When I married my husband, he slept with his arms crossed over his chest. It seemed to me he was protecting his heart; it had been wounded and broken so many times. During his waking hours, he let his guard down. But, when sleeping, he still needed to protect himself, lest some threatening force invade and attack, catching him unawares.

Joe is an early riser. Typically he gets up before I do, quietly slips out of our bedroom, exercises, makes coffee, reads the paper, and then wakes me up. Rarely do I awaken before him. But recently I did. I marveled at how peaceful he looked. He was lying on his side, one hand underneath the pillow, the other just hanging down.

His chest was wide open, not needing his protection because he finally felt safe, open, and welcoming of me. In his sleep, he reached over and wrapped his arms around me. Like two spoons in a drawer, we lay there, side by side, a perfect fit. He let me in and I was part of him, safe, next to his heart.

He's opened his heart. He trusts I won't break it.

Victoria

❦

"My sex drive isn't at its height on a usual weeknight"

Dear Reader,

It's hard to think about writing a free-flowing letter when my life seems so programmed. Don't misunderstand. It's a good life, full of kids, work, husband, endless house renovations, dogs, cat, after-school activities, friends when they can fit in, and a whole lot of family with a whole lot of issues.

So I write this on a Wednesday eve, the oldest finally in bed and asleep after many minutes of wailing because she felt I'd yelled at her. "That's how I feel," she said when I commented that I had not yelled. How can you argue with someone's feelings? The husband has retired to the bedroom to watch the baseball division playoffs, wondering but not counting on a little "nookie nookie" when I come to bed. That's a constant and amusing subject—my sex drive. "Is it that you're not interested?" my husband asks. "Is there anything that really turns you on?" he queries on a fairly regular basis.

It's not that difficult to figure out why my sex drive isn't at its height on a usual weeknight. It's up at 6:10 A.M.—press the snooze button two times for an additional ten minutes before going into overdrive for the next sixteen hours. Then it's into the shower—let the hot, hot water run on my back, which is in constant ache mode since exercise was the first thing to hit the road when work and kids and everything else took over. Soon my husband and I share our constitutional morning bathroom dialogue—what's on your agenda, can you pick up the kids, any meetings tonight? Then it's what do I wear . . .

Child no. 1 arrives with a hole in his pajamas—Superman pajamas—which he's decided to wear to preschool today. Sorry, honey, I say, but the hole is right where your penis is and it really wouldn't be good for you to go to school like that. "I'm gonna wear them anyway," he replies. Before the final chapter of this story, there are plenty of negotiations. Child no. 2 has arisen. She's in the other bathroom and says "Go away" when I ask if she needs any help. Fine with me, I'm gone.

Found an outfit, don't feel like making the bed, and just want to see if my husband will do more than simply pull up the sheets. Sheets pulled up—no complaints here. Not a good hair day. Oh, well. Breakfast, make lunches, and out the door by 7:30. One child to pre-school, one to before-school care, and parents off to work. Work, work, work. Yes, we like it. It's exhilarating, gives us mental stimulation, anxiety, satisfaction, and money.

At 5:00 P.M., pick up Child no. 1; 5:20 P.M., pick up

3

Child no. 2; 5:45 P.M., home. Backyard dug up—drainage problem. Walk around the mud and hope the yard is seeded before winter. The dogs are ecstatic to see me and the kids. Jump on the kids and make them yell and cry. Into the house, change my clothes so the silk blouse can make it through one more workday before it hits the dry cleaner, and the kids settle in for a video. Dinner—what tonight? The homemade bean and beef soup was a hit for my hubby, a bomb for the kids. How about canned soup? Yes, canned soup it is. At 7:10, upstairs and bath time. The younger one wants to be dirty for the rest of his life— dirty hair, long fingernails and toenails, the works. A minor struggle, but then into the tub. The older one is in heaven, hot water, ultimate relaxation and feeling good for a six-year-old. Bedtime around the corner after teeth brushing and pee time. Books for both kids and then . . .

It's my time. Yes, there are the dishes, the bills, the phone calls I should make to my grandmother, mother, father, brother in Detroit, mother-in-law who's making an effort to keep the barbs off the phone lines, and then a friend. God, how I love to go out with a friend and have some beers, or even better, champagne and cigarettes, and get one of those nice glows.

Full is my life. And it's my choice. I'm not sure I thought the treadmill would be this fast, though there are days when the pace slows a bit. I know I'm not a stay-at-home mom. I'd be a loony tune. I love my managerial position, my hands in a pot that makes a difference in many people's lives. Someday I'll make the time to lie in the sun, plant a small garden and weed it often enough to differentiate the plants from the weeds, ride my bike to nowhere with my husband, and find a rolling hill to lie on and just stare at the clouds rolling by.

Would I trade my life for another? No. Do I check myself at least once a week to make sure the stress level remains manageable? Yes. And so, as I feel like Superwoman and enjoy the comments others make acknowledging that I juggle a lot, I do have that inner peace of happiness.

Helena

"We are both equally convinced we are right"

Dear Reader,

Anthony was flying home from a business trip when, just to prove the seventies were not dead, the woman next to him asked, "What's your sign?"

He told her. He told her mine as well.

She shook her head at the hopelessness of it all. "A water sign and an earth sign? She's emotional, you're logical. You'll never understand each other."

When he told me the story, we laughed. To think that anyone would predict the future of our new marriage knowing nothing about us but our birthdays! He squinted at me, I bit my lip.

"We balance each other," I said.

"Right," he said, bobbing his head too hard.

Sometimes Anthony and I remind me of a couple I once saw on "The Newlywed Game."

"How far did you go before you were married?" Bob Eubanks asked.

"Third base," the wife answered promptly. Her husband said, "San Diego."

Anthony says I don't listen, get too emotional, jump to conclusions. I say he wouldn't waste so much time making decisions if he'd trust his intuition.

He says we'll never work out our differences if I don't explain my positions more rationally. I say we'll never get anywhere if he doesn't learn to take emotions—changeable, immeasurable, illogical, and very real—into account.

We are both equally convinced we are right. Perhaps we have something in common, after all.

Phoebe

"Marriage is an intensely personal journey"

Dear Reader,

My first advice is: disregard any advice you hear about marriage. Marriage is an intensely personal journey that must be negotiated internally by the partners. My rules probably wouldn't work for you nor would I want to impose external pressures on your relationship. Having said this, I'll offer some advice.

First and most important is definitely a sense of humor. A good laugh, especially at one's own foibles, can defuse a seemingly irretrievable situation. I'll never forget a particularly serious confrontation with my husband, during which, with great vigor, I pointed out his heinous behavior. When I was done with my tirade, he looked steadily at me for a moment or two and said, "I resemble that remark!" Needless to say, I lost my composure and, with it, my anger.

There is a technique that is common to couples who manage to stay together for an extended period of time. These couples navigate the dizzying ascents of the good times as well as the plummeting descents of the bad times by putting one foot in front of the other and going on every day. They simply go on. This technique appears simplistic but involves a sophisticated commitment on the part of long-term couples. They have a firm belief they're together for the duration, as they promised in their vows.

My friends and I wondered why there were so few divorces in our parents' generation. After all, they endured the depression and World War II, and those cataclysmic events and the resultant social changes could have destroyed any marriage. The difference, we decided, is our parents considered themselves married for the long term and considered divorce an option only in the most drastic circumstances.

Things are different today. Younger couples, and some older ones, consider divorce a right rather than a remedy to an intolerable situation. My husband, an attorney, has on occasion been retained by couples who were unwilling to reconcile when the offense was as trivial as "She expects me to eat dinner at her parents' house every Sunday." In most of these cases, counseling doesn't help because the individuals have been raised to believe they're entitled to have their every desire satisfied. Divorce becomes a way to avoid Mom's pot roast, a far cry from the generations who coped successfully with the greatest of life's privations.

Maybe adversity is a factor that enables spouses to sustain a long-term marriage. If so, we shouldn't be so quick to satisfy all the material needs of engaged couples. If they have to struggle, if they're hungry for the important things in life, their marriages may be strengthened. They may learn to plan and work together, qualities lacking in many younger couples today. Having shared successes and disasters, and guiding themselves by their dreams for the future, these couples may be equipped to navigate the desert times when only through hard, plodding work can they reach an oasis.

My final advice is: never underestimate the salutary effect of low expectations. Of course, this goes hand in hand with a sense of humor, but in reality this strategy concerns the concept of love in marriage. Marriage isn't about the infatuation kind of love. Rather, it's about the "I know he has dirty socks and I'm staying anyway" kind of love. Low expectations prevent us from judging our spouse's behavior too harshly. They affirm our mutual respect by acknowledging we're both human beings, doing the best we can. They keep us from feeling self-important. They let us climb mountains without heavy baggage.

If you read every word of this nonadvice, you know the first thing to do is disregard what I've said. Have fun with your life and your mate. Make your own rules. And let's meet up, at the end of our journeys, with our marriages intact. Hopefully our destination won't be a Holiday Inn where kids stay free!

Carol

"She reminded me of what's truly important"

Dear Larry,

Here it is, four in the morning, and you're about to receive a letter from your brother-in-law because your sister, or my wife, however you want to refer to her, is out of town. I never sleep well when Lily is away.

Your sister has made many impressions on me over the years and affected me in ways I'm still discovering. But the best thing she did was remind me of what's truly important. Falling more and more in love with Lily has made me realize that nothing is as important as being with her.

You're probably thinking, "Yeah, I've heard this before." But it wasn't until the night we lost the campaign, as I drove home way after midnight, that I saw, when all was said and done, that it was Lily who mattered—not my work, the campaign, or the "cause." It was Lily who would always be there for me, no matter what.

This realization liberated me. It uncluttered my mind. So I offer some observations on marriage, since you'll be getting married very shortly.

Talk to each other. I always wonder about couples who come into a restaurant, order their meals, wait, eat in silence, pay the check, and leave without engaging in

10

a discussion. Read a book and talk about it. Listen to the news and argue about what's going on. Discuss a purchase or renovation or what flowers to plant.

If one of you is a planner, make plans and agree to the ground rules. Some people go with the flow, others need goals and plans to accomplish them. We've had to remember that plans should be about dreams, not about limits. And settle the issue of children early on. Do you want them, how many, and when? Don't wait so long that you begin to feel pressure about advancing age.

Have some rituals to look forward to each week, such as watching a TV show or doing Saturday errands together or fixing her breakfast on Sunday mornings. Remember that surprises count, too. Unexpected flowers, gifts, or a night on the town keep us from getting into ruts.

Join your wife in one of her activities. It's easy to go off in another room and read or work while she's involved elsewhere in the house. Pick yourself up and become part of her life. Learn how to do what she's doing and do it with her. There's a difference between two people living with each other under the same roof and two people sharing a life together.

The sharing aspect is hardest for me. It's easier to help Lily than it is to ask for her help or disclose what's on my mind. But, believe me, if you don't make yourself vulnerable and your wife does, pretty soon she'll resent the one-sidedness of the relationship. Sharing goes both ways.

Finally, marriage isn't about reforming your partner. She brings to the table a whole lifetime of experiences that make her who she is. Every time you get upset and try to change her, you'll diminish her. I always catch myself, either right before or, usually, right after I say, "Why can't you change?" She can't, and I shouldn't ask. Instead of trying to reform her, the most important thing I can do is respect and love her.

When getting married opens up whole new possibilities and opportunities, when tolerating differences becomes the norm rather than the exception, and when the same face looks better and better as the years pass, you can be sure you have a special kind of love. Living together isn't easy. But knowing Lily is there for me beats everything. Which is why I don't get much sleep when she isn't around.

See you at your wedding.

Billy

"If I had to do it over again, I would do it over again"

Dear Reader,

How does one write about a marriage that is in its fifty-seventh year and still going strong? It is especially difficult when one's writing experience is limited to one personal letter a year and a postcard or two. Maybe the best way would be to search my memory for different incidents that would highlight what has been a truly wonderful life.

Not much money to start, so we have a stand-up wedding with just a few close friends. It is probably unbelievable by today's standards, but the first night of our honeymoon was also our first night of sex. On the second night, we were in a cabin in the Wisconsin woods and, after stories about bears, I had to stand alongside the outdoor privy with a flashlight in my hand. When we returned home after a week, we laughed about having only ten dollars to last us until the next paycheck. Silly memories, but I believe they set the basis for a close and memorable marriage.

Not much money in the early years but lots of friends, fun, and laughter. Then, when the war came, I moved my wife and three-year-old son from Chicago to Los Angeles and started a three-and-a-half-year stint in the army. Beth and Fred were able to join me for several months after I finished O.C.S. and before I left for overseas. Oh yes, the night before I went, in a weak moment, I let Beth talk me into a try for another baby. Number-two son was born nine months to the day I left for Europe.

On my return, we moved to Peoria, Illinois, with my old company. I was involved in all types of sports and, luckily for us, both sons inherited this interest. Beth was the social director and, with her smile and friendliness, involved our family in many interesting and happy activities. We next moved to Long Island and, fortunately, my progress upward in the company made it possible to have a home in the suburbs with a good high school for the boys.

Our house was a lively place, and we had a niece and nephew living with us for a number of years. The kids always had friends at the house and weekends were a time for big barbecues, which overflowed from the patio onto the lawn. The kids brought students home with them from college and, when the Forest Hills tennis matches were on, our nephew, who was a world-class tennis player, would bring five or six players to stay with us.

In 1964, I resigned after twenty-five years and we moved to Los Angeles. First Beth and I had an unforgettable four-month vacation trip through the Pacific, Hong Kong, and Japan, returning on a brand-new Greek cargo ship as the only passengers. We passed the test of togetherness and came through it loving each other and not at all bored with being on our own.

The year 1976 was the start of a new phase of our marriage. After several months of severe headaches, Beth had a ten-hour operation, as a result of which she lost her speech and became paralyzed on her right side. For a second opinion, my two sons and I took her to a famous neurosurgeon who advised us to put her in an institution, forget her, and get on with our lives.

Instead we opted for lots of love and all types of therapy—speech, occupational, physical, art, biofeedback, massage, etc. Although we were never able to eliminate the paralysis or restore her voluntary speech, we were rewarded with a very happy, outgoing, lovable individual who, with her left hand, paints beautiful, colorful pictures, which fill our house and hang in the houses and offices of our children, grandchildren, and other family members.

Looking back over these fifty-seven years, I can only say that if I had to do it over again, I would do it over again.

William

"The opposition we faced was the greatest wedding gift"

Dear Reader,

I have often thought that what helped our marriage most was that everyone was against it in the beginning.

We were introduced to each other when he was in law school, I in graduate school, both planning to spend the summer in Washington. We barely saw each other until we arrived in the new city, but June, July, and August were lovely with intimacy. In the fall we released other entanglements and, in the stressful routines of the university, depended on one another. Marriage gradually came to seem inevitable. We were adults (he was twenty-four, I twenty-three), committed to one another, ready to begin life together. What matter that his parents were Jewish and mine Protestant? Our families were much the same.

We proudly announced our engagement with a twenty-dollar turquoise ring, purchased because I thought something should mark our momentous undertaking. Then, innocent, we faced his parents, who, unreligious though they were, met our glad news with thin lips. We felt rejected, misunderstood, unappreciated.

My parents were little better. Although polite on the surface, my mother found every obstacle in the way of a wedding. An uncle was hardly civil.

And these were the relatives we heard from. We came to anticipate the anger of others—my grandmother of another generation, his aunt who celebrated each Friday with beautiful Sabbath ritual.

By spring that year, planning to marry in June, we realized ruefully that our envisioned joyful celebration, bringing a proud new law school graduate to my family and an accomplished graduate student to his, would not be as we had dreamed. My parents were unwilling to cooperate in any plans. His mother complained of the hurt to her family.

Ironically, some friends were little better. Why should I leave graduate school to marry? Why should we bother with commitment?

Before the combined weight of opposition, we were faced with an absolute choice: We could salvage life as we had known it, loving parents and grandparents, families, and communities. Or we could choose each other.

Without thinking about it very hard, we chose each other.

More than twenty years later, I see that choice as an act of unwitting wisdom. We entered marriage utterly committed to each other, already free of the strings and ties of the past.

With our decision made, events gradually turned around. A friend found a judge who happily volunteered to marry us. Faced with the possibility of her daughter's wedding going on without her, my mother decided a home ceremony would not be so bad. His parents thought perhaps a rabbi's blessing would be comforting, even if we were forbidden a Jewish ceremony. Our parents met each other cordially, discovering with pleasure that they shared common interests, bonded by an aversion to social drinking. (We had known how much they were alike, why didn't they believe us?) The wedding took place, necessary forms were upheld, and we were free to begin our life together.

Now, looking back, I think the united opposition we faced was the greatest wedding gift of all. We started our life together with our relationship a healthy, strong organism, already tested, already mature. The marriage easily has withstood the irritating lumps and bumps of living and has continued to be a haven and home for us both.

I once heard marriage described as like a base camp in mountaineering, a place from which to gather strength for the assault on the peaks and a place to return for comfort or celebration. As we've gone through life, our marriage has seemed such a base camp. From it we each have gathered the strength and confidence to face challenges that must be faced alone, knowing the marriage, the home we have made together, is utterly secure.

Now we have two children, both teenagers, a large house, two successful careers, a cat (universally recognized as exceptionally dim-witted), and a piano, among other things. My father has apologized to my husband. Both of my parents are now very close to him. Even after twenty years, his parents have not accepted our marriage, or their grandchildren. We are very happy nonetheless and look forward to at least twenty more years in each other's company.

Ellen

"I can no longer tell where he ends and where I begin"

Dear Reader,

When I met my husband, there was an uncanny sense of familiarity, as though I'd known him before. After we dated for a while, he introduced me to his parents. We were sitting in a restaurant, making polite chitchat, when I asked them where their ancestors came from. His father pronounced the name of the Russian village—Minkiewitz—and I almost fell off my chair. Minkiewitz! The same village my grandmother came from! I became convinced, at that moment, that we had indeed known each other before—in Minkiewitz.

My husband was very vocal about his feelings for me, right from the beginning. I, on the other hand, had a lousy track record with men and wasn't about to commit, verbally or otherwise. He suggested that if I couldn't say loving things in English, I might try another language. I liked the suggestion. I made verbal love to him in French, even though he didn't understand a word. He said the feelings communicated clearly across the language barrier.

One night we were lying in bed, and I looked at the open, trusting, loving face of my husband. I realized then that when someone loves you it gives you a lot of power over him (or her). If you love him back, you choose not to exercise that power. That's been a cornerstone of our marriage.

I got sick soon after my husband and I met. I had a severe biochemical disturbance and it lasted for many years. I had crippling anxiety, panic attacks, and agoraphobia. The medical community gave up on me. I lost many friends. But my husband had abiding faith in me, and I think that was what kept me from killing myself and eventually helped me get well. "The forces of light will conquer the forces of darkness," he always said. He was right.

When I was sick, I spiraled into a state of low self-esteem, and I asked my husband why he wanted to be with me, a semi-invalid. He looked at me incredulously. "I don't see you that way. Yes, you have an illness. But it isn't *you*. It's just a small part of you. To me, it's a detail."

Right from the beginning, my husband started giving me gifts. They were always extravagant and impractical. I gently talked him into giving me practical gifts, and then into smaller gifts. After a while the gifts were of no monetary value whatsoever but were just tokens of love. "You know what the greatest gift you ever gave me was?" I asked him after he brought me a dinosaur pin from a card shop. "Nope," he answered, thinking I was going to cite one of his earlier, more expensive gifts. "The greatest gift is you just accept me the way I am, and let me be." He smiled. I smiled.

In our marriage, something operates that we call "the net." We're both writers, and the net began to manifest in our work. When I'd hit a wall or get a bout of writer's block, he'd take over. When he got frustrated with one of his projects, I jumped in. We felt like we were two acrobats, and if one of us was about to fall, the other provided the net.

Now the net works in every area of our lives. If we have company and I'm too exhausted to entertain, he takes over. If something breaks in the house and he can't fix it, I figure out how to do it. We're always there for each other, holding up the net.

I mentioned before that my husband just lets me be. I wish the same were true of me. There are things about my mate that I try to change. I can't stand the fact that he goes into a deep alpha state anytime the TV is on. Many times I feel like screaming at him to shut the idiot box off, but then I realize life is a short burst, a flash of light, and I have no right to tell someone else how to spend his precious time. I back off. I leave him alone. It's something I never would have done before, something I learned from my marriage.

Sometimes someone will venture a very personal question like, "Doesn't it disturb your relationship that you earn more money than your husband?" I look at the person bizarrely, as though he or she has just posed a question in Latvian. Does it bother me that I earn more money than my husband? Why would it bother me? My husband provides the net. He helps me with all of my writing. He's my partner. He works just as hard, if not harder. So why in the world would the inequities of an arbitrary compensation system throw a monkey wrench in our marriage?

There's a strange thing about our relationship. People we don't know come up to us—in the street, in markets, at parties—and tell us how well suited we are. Is it because we both had another life together in Minkiewitz? What do other people see? I know our value systems are identical. We never have to discuss God, money, politics, friends, or a host of other subjects, because inherently we agree.

The one drawback to our marriage is that, because our lives are so busy and there's so much external stress, we don't always have the time, space, or tranquility for an active, frequent sex life. Sometimes this makes me angry and resentful. But then, when we do get together, we often have an intense experience of fusion. I've never known anything like it. There are colors and lights and then I feel a vast emptiness, a kind of black hole, that threatens to engulf me. At first I'm afraid, but then I let go, and I fall into the nothingness of cosmic completion. I can no longer tell where he ends and where I begin.

That's how much I trust my husband.

Although we share a lot of our life with friends, we have one ritual that's ours and ours alone. We bought a battered, weather-beaten old Jacuzzi and my husband restained it in redwood. We placed it under a large, circular picture window in our house. At night, before we go to bed, we hop into the Jacuzzi together. Sometimes we talk over the noise of the gurgling water and sometimes we sit, looking up at the protective moon and our cousins, the stars. We share a deep feeling of gratitude for all we have and for all the earth provides.

And then, warm and wet, hushed by awe for the created universe, we fall asleep, secure in the knowledge that we will dream side by side, and find each other there again at sunrise.

Ruth

"Marriage isn't an entitlement to change a person"

Dear Reader,

The top crust was laid in crisscrossing strips with the cherry filling peeking out. I'd never seen a pie that didn't have a nice, complete pie crust. It was cherry pie alright, but it was strange. It was Father Glynn's cherry pie. I was five and he was cooking in our kitchen in Rhode Island. This was back in the late fifties, and parish priests still visited their congregations' kitchens back then.

I knew very little about Father Glynn beyond his pie crust because he left to head up a parish in his native Canada shortly thereafter. However, to a five-year-old who'd experienced no pie crusts other than nice, complete ones, his was a heresy. I just couldn't get used to it. I never have.

I next saw Father Glynn when I was eighteen and my parents asked him to officiate at my brother's wedding in Montreal. At the sermon for the wedding, Father Glynn said most people make a grave mistake in their marriages: The husband and wife try to change each other. Fix the spouse's faults. Modify the spouse's habits. Complain when change in the spouse isn't forthcoming.

Father Glynn said while people change greatly over the course of their lives, their capacity to direct and control change within themselves is limited. Yes, you try to gain self-knowledge, stop doing certain things you do, and start doing other things you didn't do. But, he warned, the relative permanence of personality means attempts to control change generally fail. Given your own general incapacity to change, it's perverse to try to cause your spouse to change.

Father Glynn told my brother and his wife that although they were happy then, there would be many days when they would be upset at each other. When they might even hate each other. They should realize and accept this and not try to change each other in order to improve their marriage. Trying to change your spouse will compound the problems that arise in even a happy marriage, he said, and will cause discord and animosity. Marry your spouse for the person he or she is, not for the person you would have him or her be. Because *you* married your spouse, your spouse by definition is not the problem. If he or she is wrong for you, it's your problem. If he or she is wrong for you, admit it to yourself. Marriage isn't an entitlement to change another person.

After the ceremony, people were saying this was a crazy sermon. It seemed on point to me, having witnessed my parents' lack of success as mutual change agents. I didn't engage in rebuttal, though, as I had to spend most of my time avoiding the entreaties of a bridesmaid from northern Ontario who didn't interest me, even after she went to her father for help. Her father asked why I was ignoring her. Didn't I like girls? They were crazy, I thought, not Father Glynn.

Eight years later, I asked Father Glynn to co-officiate at my wedding. (No, my wife doesn't hail from northern Ontario.) I asked him to give the same sermon at my wedding, and to my pleasure, he complied. He also told an off-color joke at our reception afterward. I can't repeat it here.

Fourteen years later, our marriage is no better than most, although our kids and our careers keep us from obsessing too much about each other's heresies. Heresies in the sense of cherry pie with the wrong crust, and all the other things I do that she can't accept. And vice versa. And since she can't accept them, she complains and tries to change me. And vice versa. Sometimes these pie crust arguments become overcrisp. And then we realize we're not arguing over the filling, and we disengage. To engage again too often.

Father Glynn was right. Which is probably why he never married.

George

26

"Since then we've changed our lives again"

Dear Reader,

Jane left me early in April 1975. She took one of the cars—a chartreuse two-seater—and some clothes and drove to Washington, where she moved into a studio apartment near National Airport and went to work managing a congressman's Capitol office.

I got to keep the sedan, the dog, the house, and the sometime company of our youngest son, who came home for the summer from college.

Here's how—and why, I think—it happened. We'd been married for twenty-nine years, living in Levittown for the last twenty-three of them while we raised two boys. The older one was working and living on his own. We were able to send the younger one to a good, small, fairly expensive school only because Jane doubled her twenty hours a week working in the congressman's local office.

There had been a crisis or two during our marriage, but they had been completely resolved years before Jane left me. We loved each other very much, but I think we were both bored to death with suburban life, especially since we were now empty nesters. We needed a change,

27

a real change in the way we lived. Jane, I'm sure, needed it even more than I did.

When one of the top spots in the congressman's Washington office opened up, and he offered it to her, she told me, "I want it."

"Don't be ridiculous," I said.

"Oh, please, let's think about it. You wouldn't be alone. The dog's here. And Mike will be home all summer. I could come home on weekends. You could come to Washington sometimes. I'm so excited!"

I was feeling a little nervous. And a little interested.

"Wait a minute," I said. "How long are you talking about? Jesus, I can't believe you're serious."

"Who knows? Maybe I'll hate it and come back next week. Maybe we'll both love it for a while. I've got to try it, darling. I've never wanted anything so much in my life."

I could see that. I began to be worried, jealous, frightened . . . and excited myself. So I agreed, and she went.

The six months Jane spent in Washington were among the absolutely best six months of our lives. I flew down almost every Friday night (took the train once, but it was much too slow), and our weekends were full of wonders. We explored every museum of the

Smithsonian, ate marvelous meals, made incredible love, endured unendurable Washington heat, toured the White House, the Capitol, and all the rest, and parted very, very sadly every Sunday night.

Back in Levittown I went to work, somehow got meals together for Mike and me, walked the dog, declined most social invitations from our friends, and looked forward to the next glorious weekend.

After six months on her own in the very innards of government, Jane realized she missed me and her friends and some of her previous life too much to stay any longer. We decided that adventure was over, but we knew what it had done for our relationship and our lives would never be over.

In September our son Jake and I drove down in his van, loaded up all of Jane's stuff (by then she'd sold the two-seater), and drove back home through a major rainstorm.

The end? No, it was only the start of our change. In February we moved back to Manhattan, where we'd lived for a few months after our marriage, and lived a different, fantastically happy life for ten years.

Since then we've changed our lives again, because changing is what you have to do.

Phil

"Andre helped take away the loneliness"

Dear Reader,

Andre is my home. He gives me back the days when I was a child and ran home from school and couldn't get home fast enough 'cause my mom was not at work, she was home, and my favorite things would be cooking and the house would be neat and warm.

Andre chased away my boogeymen—'cause he laughs and makes me laugh—'cause he knows enjoying life, not worrying about it, is important.

I met Andre right after I said to myself, "I couldn't live with anyone again. I like my solitude, my home. I've finally made peace with my life. I'm older now. I don't think I can do it again."

Ten years younger than I am, Andre made me laugh—rearranged my home and helped take away the loneliness I'd felt all my life. The age difference doesn't matter.

Andre has a child whom I adore and daydream about. She's so lovely. Since I can't have children, every-thing just fell into place—as if it was meant to be.

Life is easier and less scary now that there are two of us. In fact, I find less need for other people. As I said,

Andre is my home. Together we have created a life with all the best parts, and the missing parts, of the homes we had as children. I feel we were meant to be. Who he is is what I need, and I think it's the same for him.

Linda

"Memories are all we truly own"

Dear Reader,

The circumstances surrounding the death of a spouse are so unique, they are spiritual moments in and of themselves. I know. I went through this experience with my wife, and I hope this recollection helps others brave their storms.

After Helen and I were married, we chose not to have children. As a result, we were able to travel extensively and enjoyed the fine arts in many cities around this country. Helen was a nurse who changed careers to become an English professor. My work is advertising research. However, my volunteer activity is grief and bereavement counseling, which I worked at for five years before our own tragedy struck. I guess, in a way, I was prepared.

In 1991, after sixteen years of marriage, Helen did not feel well on a trip, asked to see a gastroenterologist, and was told it was likely that ovarian cysts were pushing against her intestines. Three weeks later, after nine hours of surgery, the doctors knew the cysts were ovarian cancer.

I know how hard it is for doctors to admit a disease has won. When I was called into the examining room to join Helen, I saw two boxes of tissue and knew the game was over. The doctor did not have to say anything. Knowing Helen had been a nurse, he showed us two chest X rays, one from her first visit three weeks before, the other from that morning. She read her own X rays. The ovarian cancer had jumped to her chest and was taking over her lungs. She, too, had little to say.

In hospice training, I was taught how to deal effectively with the terminally ill patient and the family. The training did not prepare me to be with someone, especially my wife, at the precise moment she learned she would soon die.

It was a long drive back to our home, holding hands and crying and realizing we might have weeks, or maybe a month or so, but definitely not much more time together. The whole meaning of our lives took shape for us, and we saw what was important and what was not.

For a few weeks, Helen was somewhat ambulatory, as long as we took the portable oxygen unit. She lasted nine months. One Sunday, close to the end, Helen asked to go for a ride. I thought she wanted to see the coast, but she really wanted to go to the cemetery and stand in her space. I had read about acceptance but had never seen it so vividly demonstrated.

After she died, and time went by, I found it difficult to decide when and how to remove my wedding band. I talked this over with an associate who had helped me with my grief, and he pointed out that rituals help at times like these. Since there was no such ritual in religious literature, he suggested I propose one, and I did.

My experiences with my wife both amplified and replaced what I had been taught about terminally ill patients and their families. Sometimes people who know my training ask me how I deal with hallmark events like birthdays, anniversaries, holidays. I tell them what I find hard is dealing with unexpected events that are significant, especially when it is difficult to talk about them. For example, I am remarried now and try to limit what I say about my first marriage. On four occasions, my new family and I have driven past the location where Helen and I learned she was dying. Part of me wants to say something, yet I think I have to keep my feelings inside. If my new wife admires a particularly beautiful place, one that Helen, as an environmentalist, fought to preserve, and it reminds me of her, I do not say anything.

My new family and I recently moved, and as I cleaned and packed, I found some of Helen's belongings.

One of her hobbies was painting, so I put two of her paintings in my office. I found two good photos of her and put them away. Then I found her Ph.D. diploma. Was it really more than a piece of paper? I kept wondering. So many symbolic objects have reverted to "things" since she is gone. I decided to send her diploma to her sister. Perhaps it will inspire someone else to study hard.

When Helen hit her stride, she was the leader of a major environmental organization. She started at the local level and went on to the state level and then to the national committees. This environmental group purchased a memorial stone for the foot of the grave site and planted wildflowers and endangered species of plants around it. For her headstone I chose an inscription from folk literature. To me it says a lot about the meaning of life. The inscription reads, "Memories are all we truly own."

> *Benjamin*

"We were on automatic"

Dear Reader,

I read an article recently about regrets, and I saved it. I have regrets about my married life. My husband died a year ago after a long illness. He was in his mid-forties.

Before he became ill, we were so caught up in daily living we lost sight of the big picture. We sort of lost ourselves in dealing with everyday life and responsibilities. Our daughters, the apartment, work—these were all diversions that kept us from concentrating on our relationship. Getting everything else settled was more important. We were on automatic and our relationship wasn't as good as it could have been had we worked at it. We let it slide. We thought we would have more time.

It's difficult to make a success of a marriage and wonderful when it happens. We could have had a great marriage, but we let it go. Now I know what I missed, and my fear is I won't have another opportunity.

Marriage has its peaks and valleys. I miss it.

Abigail

"I'm still very much in love with my wife"

Dear Reader,

I'm still very much in love with my wife. We're a lot older now, droopier in several places, and often tired from the day, or our responsibilities, and the rush of three kids. We're still attracted to each other physically, but we don't attempt, or don't get, the chance to show it as

35

often—or as spontaneously—as we once did. Although we did recently resort to getting a baby-sitter and parking in our own car by the lake, just for the chance to touch and be close without the threat of interruption.

We've been married fourteen years. We have three children. Two of their births were close calls. Our middle child wasn't breathing when he was born, and the nurses struggled—for some time—to revive him. Thank God they succeeded. We battled my wife's severe cancer for two years after the birth of our first child. We've moved around a bit, out of the country once for two years, around the United States three or four times. We've studied together and apart, started new jobs, cultivated two careers, made new friends, explored new places, found them interesting, sometimes boring, but they were all new experiences for us, and we shared them together. And we grew and struggled together and have succeeded in our endeavors, I guess.

Now we're very busy. It seems we both have a lot to do, have a lot of responsibilities, and both do a pretty good job. But we work late, drive kids to practice and friends' houses, have to speak on the infernal phone, and are frequently out at night. Occasionally we sit down to look into each other's eyes and remember all we've been through, what we've accomplished, and what we have to look forward to. But we don't do this very often. I suppose our biggest issue is time—balancing responsibilities and schedules, and being able to remember our marriage and our love, and to work at it.

We know all the things we should do to work at our marriage and budget our time, but only occasionally do we get to them. Even so, my wife's been the one constant in my life, and she's become the center of my life. I think she feels the same about me. I hope this doesn't mean we take each other for granted. Rather, history, and being equal to or surviving a number of surprises and challenges, has helped cement our love—even when it means a note to that effect affixed to the refrigerator, gradually sliding to a forty-five-degree angle.

I can honestly say that I love my wife more now than I did when we married. I certainly know her better. I've seen her in a million different situations and we've shared and accomplished some wonderful things. My most romantic fantasy is that someday soon we'll have long hours to sit in a cozy café and waste time and talk about everything we want to talk about, go for a walk, then take a nap together. It may not be erotic, but it's the thing I long for with the one I've come to love more and more over the years. I think she loves me too. There's a note on the fridge that says so.

Tom

"We choose partners for many reasons"

Dear Reader,

My dad was fifteen years older than my mother. For various reasons (some dramatic, some melodramatic), I did not meet him until I was nine. At twelve I was sent to camp (the one and only time), and the man most interested in me was fifteen years my senior. As we danced, I kept wishing he would remove the "ball" from his pocket, but I never had the courage to ask him to do so. At sixteen I was madly in love with a boy a year older than I, but the one who loved me was a man twelve years my senior. At nineteen I met the man I was to marry. He was twenty years older and asked me to agree to "be the flexible one," to change when change was needed, because I would always be the younger, he the wiser. I agreed. I honored our agreement for our first twenty-five years and recanted for the last ten.

Now my mother tells me, too late, that I was always special, had a different vision of people and events, and would have become the person I am no matter who was in my life. I credit my husband for any intellectual acumen I possess. I credit him for teaching me to see nature. A walk with him in Central Park was a memorable experience. He loved the beauty of pebbles, the complexities of leaves (he taught me to distinguish some twenty varieties), the patterns of trees against the sky. Literature, music, history, politics, seeing the larger picture—the list seems endless.

Some things were always mine. The ability to love, trust, and touch, to see beyond what people said, to understand and comfort. My need to surround my family in warmth as well as beauty was preeminent. My love of art was consuming, and mine always. It was my eye he sought regarding aesthetics, value, and authenticity. When he needed another opinion on human reactions, feelings, and undertones, it was my sensibility he respected.

My husband was a powerful intellectual admired by other intellectuals. My role in this milieu was to listen, learn, and appreciate. He was not powerful in the ability to love, give, be sociable, and function in the everyday world. I was the caregiver, the money manager, the party giver, the friend maker, the homemaker, and my husband's guardian. All very powerful roles. His absolute need for me to be powerful so the household could function, along with his absolute need for me to seem docile, subordinate, and certainly less than equal in our marriage, was at first somewhat acceptable, a few years later less acceptable, and in future years infuriating.

As the children grew, we fought—should they be

allowed to talk at dinner, must our daughter always be in dresses, how much responsibility should be theirs, how quiet do they have to be so Father may sleep late—and Camelot began to shake. When I was not allowed to pursue my interests by myself but had to wait for my husband to share them with me, when the past caught up with the present, when togetherness became imprisonment, Camelot trembled.

At forty, I read *Passages*. I was ready and Gail Sheehy talked right at me. I lost sixty pounds and began to talk about rejoining the work force. He said, "Nothing doing. Our agreement twenty-one years ago was you would stay home for me and the children forever." When he asked for whom I had lost all the weight, and I answered, "For me," he did not speak to me for a day. When he did, he said it would have been polite if I had lied to make him feel better. Camelot crumbled.

A rereading of this letter screams both truths and omissions.

Yes, we choose partners for many reasons. Mine were as complex and numerous as yours might be. I foresaw many of the problems I would face in a shared life with him—his need to control, lack of regard for money, constant illnesses, possessiveness, alienation, and his inability to compromise with the academic world. Yet when the opportunity came to marry someone else, I turned it down cold. He was what I wanted. I chose a life partner who could fulfill my most important needs. Why then blame him for what he did or could not do?

All my life I have striven to fail at success. Winning both thrills and scares me, compliments delight and embarrass me, approaching success screams danger. For most of my life I chose oblivion. My first serious commitment was to my husband and children. I found pride in my husband's intellect and comfort in his enormous need for my love and strength. Our attachment to each other was immense. I pulled away at great cost to both of us. I grew into my own person at great cost to him. By the time he died, bitterness and anger were constant companions in our marriage. I now wish we had both been wiser, kinder, and more flexible, because we had something extremely special.

He did show me beauty, even though I had it in me too. He did make learning a special joy, though I always loved to learn. He did love us, though loving was easier for me. He was giving, though he needed so much.

Without him now, I have encountered freedom I have never known before. Without fear I experience being alone, making choices, sharing time with our children and friends, making plans for my future, redecorating my home and my life.

I miss him and love him. He is still "the singing

master of my soul" and I feel privileged to have shared a life with him.

Having said this, I find myself looking forward to the years ahead, alone or with another. The essentials have changed, the absolutes are better understood, fear is checked, self-esteem is within grasp, and aspirations for a shared life are fulfilled.

Suzanne

"I was angry at myself for having pushed her so far"

Dear Reader,

When I first married, I was filled with the craziest notions: There is only one head of the household—the man. The wife is supposed to stay home and be a housewife. Women do not have careers. Men should make more money than women.

These are lousy values to start out with. Nevertheless, they were mine, and I pursued them with vigor. I didn't realize that by believing in these values, I was forcing my wife into a subservient role. We argued about my late hours, my social drinking, and the other reasons I was prevented from being with her. I couldn't get her to realize that these were sacrifices I was making for our marriage and that she would just have to be patient. I was so impressed with my importance, I couldn't see her point of view. Basically, I didn't value my wife as an equal.

Then one day, after I returned from a four-day fishing trip with my father, she and I had another argument about our roles as husband and wife. I'm not sure why, but this time I actually started to listen to her. Upon reflection, it was humiliating to see the woman I loved, tears running down her face, just asking for my recognition. I remember how angry I was with myself for having pushed her so far.

What caused me to change? I think it was friendship. During our four-year courtship, my fiancée became my best friend. She still is, and it was because of our friendship that I wanted her tears to stop.

I started listening more, and things started to get a whole lot better. I began to see a pattern emerging. I started to recognize the value of a shared life based on mutual respect. This implies honesty, integrity, morality, compassion, sympathy, and cooperation. I feel very strongly that true friendship is the key to a successful marriage because after the fire cools—and it always does—you still have your best friend. And true friendship lasts forever.

Jeff

❦

"Marriage falls easily into dangerous tedium"

Dear Reader,

I don't claim to know much about sailing, but I know in my marriage I'm always "tacking"—trying hard to keep the wind in the sails, working to move forward on a course that's never straight. Sometimes there's no course at all.

My marriage, and observing my friends, has led me to define three pet areas of difficulty: How do we allow ourselves and each other to change? How can we avoid assuming roles that are counterproductive? And how can we move past our feelings in order to care more for our mates?

I, for one, worship change—the way it reveals itself in the world around us, the way it occurs within me. In fact, I can't tolerate much repetition, preferring untried restaurants, unknown shores, new people. Marriage falls easily into dangerous tedium. It's built into the institution, but we also create it, largely by the lazy habit of not acknowledging change in each other or in our relationships.

We claim to want change but then insist the other person be the way he was, not the way he is. We don't see changes that occur in ourselves, either—much like the fat person who loses forty pounds and still sees himself as fat. We hold each other back from unfolding naturally, as if marriage were a commitment to stay the same forever. This behavior, alarmingly commonplace, is foolish, stubborn, and blind.

People change—and if these changes pull the couple apart, they need to be acknowledged and maybe even celebrated. Why can't married people be like two planets that turn on their own axes while rotating around each other, pulled together at times, apart at others? Do we have to share the same game plan? Isn't mutual respect enough? Shouldn't the marriage vow be "I support your fulfillment"?

Not only do I value change, I value freedom. This isn't selfish. Actually, it's generous. I want textured fullness with dimensions and flexibility. I want it for the marriage and for each of us. I don't want something constructed and brittle, something that snaps in two when the strong winds blow. I don't want a relationship that's stuck, no wind in the sails, becalmed.

As Freud observed, couples find themselves in the porcupine's predicament. That is, we need to draw close for warmth but not so close that we hurt each other. The key is to stop holding on to each other so tightly—to have faith in the notion that the more we let each other go, the more likely we'll remain together and share more, as vital, awake people.

Can we please also stop falling into easy roles, too

clichéd to be tolerable? Can women stop mothering their husbands? Creating little boys out of men is counterproductive. Instead we can be guides, bringing wisdom and intuition, which tends to be more in the fiber of our beings than theirs. This is a gift women have—use it or lose it, as the saying goes.

Our job in each other's lives isn't to busy ourselves filling each other's gaps. It's to guide each other toward filling our own gaps. Some people genuinely complement each other, without effort or sacrifice. But when this happens out of mutual *need*, anger is never too far beneath the surface. As a friend once said to me, "Rain makes plants grow. Dew makes plants want to grow." We should be "dew" to each other, then. Our work is in fulfilling our lives individually, together.

Finally, I work to care for my husband rather than getting caught in my feelings. Feelings change all the time—*they're simply feelings*. I don't suggest we ignore or eliminate them. No, I mean we need to be sensitive to how transitory they are. Feelings are constraining when we place too much importance on them. In my own case, beneath frequent feelings of anger, frustration, and sadness there's another level of deep friendship and abiding love.

There are calm waters out beyond the waves. Can we reside there? Can I?

Diana

"Our marriage continues to demand the best from us"

Dear Reader,

I have come to understand that a good marriage compels compromises that are not considered in more problematic marriages. When responsibility to the partnership equals in importance responsibility to oneself, there is pressure—a constant juggling of priorities and time.

When I married for the second time, I was forty. I knew I was marrying the only man to whom I could make this commitment, the only man for whom I could have enough love and trust and respect. Even so, after taking my marriage vows, I lost my voice for five to six weeks. I was unconsciously afraid of marriage, or my perception of marriage, which, while it included all the wonders of unified love, did not have much to do with individual growth.

The ensuing years have been lessons in the give and take individual growth requires—the hesitancy, the guilt, the acceptance as we both learn to let go of old patterns and adjust to and support new ones. As we have matured in our understanding, our marriage has grown stronger, until I can no longer imagine myself unmarried. Nevertheless, my marriage continues to set the parameters within which I grow, at times frustrated and chafing against its limitations.

These limitations have earned my respect because my marriage is important to me. The sacrifices and compromises I make to preserve unity have benefited me spiritually and I believe I am a better person because of it. Personal ambitions and ego have become less important than an open and loving heart and letting go of anger and blame.

Feeling misunderstood has forced me to better understand myself. Sharing time has taught me to value time. My good marriage has enriched and sustained me as I have enriched and sustained it.

Marriages without love and respect, marriages unvalued, can easily ignore needed compromises, while preservation of the ego-self seems essential. Under these circumstances the marriage is viewed as a devouring monster. Needless to say, a marriage must be valued equally by both partners for it to be harmonious, and this harmony is subject to change.

Recently I have found myself growing toward a different lifestyle vision, one that I would find more nurturing and compatible with a deepening spiritual commitment to myself, my family, and my environment. Perhaps this has always been at the end of my rainbow, and now, at age fifty-five, it is glowing brighter. It would require major changes from our current circumstances, but this feeling is too right to be ignored. I have discussed this with my husband and have secured a promise that we will work toward this future together.

The poet/artist/dreamer within me clearly understands that my present happiness and future dreams include a magic that encompasses more than myself, and so the patient prioritizing and compromising will go on as our marriage continues to demand the best from both of us.

A good marriage is perhaps a metaphor for social unity and responsibility, a belief in the oneness of all things that will lead us to peace.

Anne

"I wanted so much from my marriage"

Dear Reader,

When I think of marriage, I think of planning and preparing Christmas dinner only to learn on Christmas Eve that the boys were all going to their mother's. I guess someone forgot to tell me. My husband, an avid racquetball player, was also occupied on Christmas. I remember sitting alone on the couch, wondering where I was, why I was there, and how in the world I was going to survive.

The first Mother's Day came and I was filled with anxiety. We went to church, where a gift was given to the mother with the most children. I prayed the number four wouldn't turn up. Was I a mother? Do stepmothers count? Fortunately, a mother with more children happily knew she was a mother and stood up to receive the gift. Later, at lunch, a close friend, who knew of my desire to be part of a family, toasted all the mothers at our table. Several couples had gathered at a restaurant after church, and as he went around the table lifting his glass and naming each one, I felt the anxiety build. Sure enough, he came to me, passed me over, and went on to toast the next mother. I guess that answered my question. No, stepmothers don't count.

I had noticed that. I had also noticed that I did most of the motherly things—the cleaning up, taxi service, grocery-buying, food preparation, teacher conference, birthday-celebration-planning kinds of things. The boys were glad I ran errands for them and provided extra money for things they wanted, but they weren't interested in me as a confidante, they weren't interested in me as a mother. I never got the hugs and the times of joyful remembrances that even teenage boys are willing to grant their mom, at least on rare occasions.

I wanted so much from my marriage. I wanted to be part of a loving family. I wanted to be accepted and valued as a friend, realizing I would never be a mother. I also wanted the fun times of courtship to continue. I had a fantasy of what life could be like. There was lots of evidence my fantasy would never materialize, but I didn't pay attention to the evidence. I wasn't clear about what I wanted and expected. My husband wasn't clear about what he wanted and expected, and the boys were just hopeful it would be good but probably had lots of concerns that were never voiced and addressed.

It should be obvious that marriage, especially a stepfamily situation, is going to be hard work. But somehow it wasn't obvious to us. My husband and I lived very independent lives. We each had our careers and we spent lots of time apart. The problem was that there was such loneliness, such lack of connection. Instead of closeness there was television. Hours and hours of television. In the first year of our marriage, we never had one night alone in the house, and the evenings of quiet dinners and long conversations we had enjoyed before marriage were gone.

My spiritual life was both a help and a hindrance. I would turn to prayer, meditation, and spiritual reading for solace. I would move into a larger perspective and seek to surrender myself to a high spiritual good that might be served through my presence in the family. The problem was, instead of really transforming the pain and anger, I was repressing it in the name of a misunderstood spiritual humility. I was sacrificing myself physically by failing to recognize that God didn't want me to be treated as a doormat. The children were precious to God, but so was I.

Now I realize how careful women must be not to take such positive values as spiritual humility and service to others and misapply them. Motherhood, whether biological or not, requires sacrifice. But to allow Spirit to move in our lives on behalf of ourselves and others, we must be healthy. We must take care of ourselves, physically, mentally, and emotionally, to have the strength to sacrifice some of our personal preferences and choices to meet the needs of others. We have to learn how to establish appropriate boundaries for ourselves and respect them. By taking care of ourselves, we model healthy behaviors for our children, too.

I'm no longer in this family. We finally went through a very civilized divorce. No angry words. Only a recognition on both our parts that it wasn't working. We weren't prepared for the challenges, and when the challenges came, our coping mechanisms were sadly deficient. We tended to avoid conflict, be gone longer from home, spend time with friends outside the marriage, and stay very busy. Whenever there were good times, and there were many, we pretended all of the bad times were resolved. Not only did we not deal with the issues, we failed to teach the boys how to deal with issues. Now they're in their own marriages, and I feel sadly sure they're repeating our errors.

When I think back on those long years, I remember very little. But the pain and anger are still in my body. I gave ten years of my life—critical, childbearing years—trying to create a family that was not to be and forgoing the opportunity to form a healthy partnership with a man and raise a family of my own. The opportunity for me to have children is now gone. The opportunity for a happy marriage is, however, still mine.

My hope is that I can find ways of unearthing the pain and freeing the rivers of love and joy that have been dammed up by my efforts to ignore the truth about myself and my marriage. The work is hard, but the possibility of what can come from it motivates me. At the end of the tunnel is light, and I think the light is life—creative, joyful (though not conflict-free) life.

Patricia

"Being a stepmother has enriched my life"

Dear Reader,

There must be a politically correct phrase for "stepmother." I've always hated this word. Perhaps "alternative mother," "additional mother," or "other mother" would do. As a child, I loved the Disney movies, but when I married, the stepmothers in *Cinderella* and *Snow White* became my enemies. Disney portrayed them as evil incarnate, and the image stuck.

Precisely sixteen years ago, I joined the ranks of "additional mothers." Although my husband's divorce was not the most pleasant experience, he and his ex-wife (another term I have come to loathe) vowed to minimize the stress on their two girls.

It was hard. Two adults, no longer in love, barely able to speak civilly to one another, must appear cordial in public and pretend to the girls that they belong in both homes. But no matter how hard they tried, both homes were different. Even the rules were different.

Enter the New Wife. The Stepmother.

I tried, I really did. I was in my twenties, blindly in love with a divorced man with two small children. My parents were upset: even his parents weren't thrilled about his remarrying so soon after the divorce.

The girls and I got along fine. But we all had to learn how to share Daddy. I remember going to the movies with the family and trying not to be angry when one or both children wanted to sit in the middle or on Daddy's lap.

I made a supreme effort, although my hands would

shake and my heart pound, when we all joined at some school event. I smiled a lot. But I always had to move one step back so that their mother could acknowledge the girls' accomplishments and express her pleasure. Sometimes I was overlooked. Sometimes the girls forgot to introduce me. Sometimes I found myself explaining to strangers who I was and why I was there. To avoid the word "stepdaughters," the words I usually used were "my husband's daughters." But it took a few extra seconds to say it, and by then no one was listening.

I had to understand that when there were only two tickets to a school event, I wasn't the first choice. When there were doctor or dentist appointments, I wasn't the one immediately selected to represent the family.

I tried not to be resentful of alimony, those monthly payments in addition to child support payments that are due at the first of the month, no matter what. I can look back on those obligations fondly now because they've been replaced by college tuition and loans.

I learned some limits: Never discipline the children. Try really hard not to complain to your spouse about them. Don't argue in front of the children, lest their mother learn of it. Don't ask many questions about their mother, lest they become defensive and hostile.

I always lived in dread of The Phrase. I thought I was prepared, but one night it happened. I finally had it flung at me, twelve years into our marriage, in a moment of teenage hysteria. My husband was on a business trip and the younger daughter, then fifteen and angry with something I did or said, yelled, "You cannot tell me what to do. You are not my mother!" I did what any responsible thirty-six-year-old woman would do. I burst into tears.

For me, the most significant change in my relationship with the girls took place when I became a mother. They were teenagers by the time our daughter was born. They were there at her birth. They held and kissed her. And never once did I apply another dreaded phrase to the older girls, "half-sisters." They're sisters. And I pray that when my daughter grows up and her parents aren't there for her, she'll have the love and affection of her two older sisters to guide her.

As a mother, I realize now how hard it must have been for their mother to smile through family events. I don't think twice about my daughter sitting in between her parents or waking up in the night wanting reassurance. When she asks for her own set of house keys, I wouldn't hesitate. I would sacrifice anything for her college tuition.

At twenty and twenty-three, the older girls are women now. The oldest has a job and her own apartment nearby. We helped her move. We cleaned the apartment—on a different day than her mom. She comes over more often now than when we had visiting privileges. She even gave us her house keys for emergencies.

Being a stepmother has enriched my life. I don't expect the girls to love me as much as their mother, but when they say, "I love you," I know it comes from a very special place in their hearts, as it does in mine.

Jane

"Our love has many faces"

Dear Reader,

It was nearly twenty-one years ago that we made those promises before God, the pastor, and the whole company there gathered. The words were "to love, honor, and cherish . . . in sickness and health . . . for richer, for poorer, and in all life's realities . . . until death parts us." These words have been the anchor that has held us through these years. They've proven, these promises, to be our security, trust, source of perseverance, the foundation and definition of our love through the many trials that have been "all life's realities."

We started out a couple of kids. My grad school cost

a fortune at that time. Our first rent was $75 a month, chicken cost 22 cents a pound, my wife's full-time salary was $325 a month, we fed ourselves on $29 a week. We were broke, married, in love, and, for the greatest amount of time, happy.

We've had to make our own way, create our own marriage out of the dreams and images of what we want our lives to be. We didn't have much of a blueprint to follow. We were both born into families steeped in alcoholism and our parents' marriages were less than enviable. We've been tossed between relief at being far from their continuing problems and insecurity about being on our own. The traits we both inherited have been some of the greatest obstacles we've had to overcome. We've struggled with being depressed and withdrawing into guarded feelings and loneliness. There were confusing times when we were tempted to pack the car and head back to the insanity we knew because it seemed less frightening than the future we were carving out for ourselves.

We fought, we cried, we made up, and we made it from day to day. We were determined that our family would be different, our children would avoid our experiences. So we set out together on a wing and a prayer.

One of my greatest regrets is that marriage and children don't come with books of instruction. Ah, yes, children. Our first arrived with a fanfare. After two years of marriage, using multiple means of birth control, the stork arrived with a little girl. She took thirty-two hours to come into the world and made her grand entrance butt first. We went from childhood to parenthood in one fell swoop. I didn't know what panic was until we walked the floors those sleepless nights before figuring out the colic was due to a milk allergy. We learned how to cry between bouts of pleading with God to let us switch places with our poor little girl.

Our second arrived four years later, this one planned, another little girl. She came with a lot less effort. Life has a funny twist about it. The child who came with such difficulty grew strong. The one who came so easily has now at fourteen faced her own mortality at least twenty times as we've rushed her to the emergency room during asthma attacks. We've learned again what fear is while waiting in pediatric intensive care to find out if she'll make it.

The "how to's" and "don'ts" have unfolded with every day of experience as together we've stopped, made decisions, and refined and shaped the lives we've wanted. After twenty-one years together, our work still isn't finished, though much of its beauty has come to the surface. We've hit the midlife time of our lives. Our rent is $600 a month, chicken costs $1.39 a pound, and my wife earns considerably more than the $325 she was paid when we started out. I've been working for thirteen years. Now forty, my wife has graduated from college, buried her mother, who died suddenly, and is about to dance in her first recital. We have one daughter in college, one about to enter high school. There's a pattern to our lives that will help our children as they form and shape their own lives. We're still broke, still married, still in love, and much happier than we've ever been.

We come back to the beginning, to those promises. Those words are where we began, before the altar. There was no magic in the words, no hocus pocus, there were no great secrets to be found but this one: We believed in what we were doing. We believed in a God who made promises to us about his love and faithfulness. We believed that we and our hopes and dreams were worth every effort. We believed, and still believe, that what we have is worth having.

Our love has changed many times in these years. Love has meant, and still means, butterflies in the stomach and silly grins and giggles and playful caresses, little secrets whispered in each other's ears. Love has meant time spent listening to pain left over from the years of growing up, words that hurt when they lead to uncomfortable self-perceptions. There were times when love has meant having to say "I'm sorry" many times over because problems took years to fix. It has meant taking next steps not knowing the outcome, allowing time and space for one of us to heal before we could go on to something new.

Our love has had many faces: joyous, meek, playful, some with uncertain tears. Our love has had the face of youthful romance and the maturity of willful persistence to endure the pain of rock bottom. We've endured because we've always come back to the foundation that brought us together in the first place—our love. We've been able to allow our love to grow and change into what it needed to be for the time. Our promises have stood inviolate, giving us strength during the worst times and pleasure during the best.

Ray

"The example we set for our children is their legacy"

Dear Reader,

During the seventies, when drugs and free love were the norm, recently divorced after a fifteen-year marriage, I met Julia while I was working out of state. We fell very much in love. When the job was finished, I returned to Denver and we carried on our relationship over the phone and on weekends. She was a special kind of lady, well-educated, beautiful, gracious, curious, and searching—typical for that time. After a little less than a year, she moved to Denver and we lived together. Together we were a team, ready to take on the world.

During our first year together, my ex-wife, who had fought for custody and won, decided to give up our children. So I took over the raising of five kids, ages fourteen to six, and hoped my lady would help me with them. We were now a family, or so I thought at the time.

My career was in full swing, and I had more work than I could handle. My job kept me on the road several months at a time, about six months a year. When Julia came with me it was all new, plenty to do, plenty of excitement for her. We had many common bonds, were the best of friends, and just liked being and traveling together. We traveled around the world together, working, and those times were the greatest.

I wanted her to be with me, and I was proud to have her by my side. She preferred this to the role of step-mother, so we left the kids with sitters at home. While we did the We thing, my children started wondering who was going to be there for them.

A few years into the relationship, I became aware that I was not the only man in Julia's life. Julia had two lives and believed nobody knew about the other. She was away from home an average of two months a year, whether at a retreat, studying drama in another city, or visiting her family and old friends, away from the children and the responsibilities that came with raising them. My love for her was very strong, so I decided to put up with her searching even while I hoped she would settle down and take a greater role in my family. She found it necessary to search, and the searches always found her a new man of the moment. Not until the end of our relationship would I tell her I knew about the other men. I hid my jealousy and anger because, in the free love of the seventies, you did not judge.

Eventually Julia's agenda changed. She believed it was right for her to have an alternate lifestyle and started using drugs and Indian folklore to bring her closer to God. Drugs began to play a major role in my life, too; we did a lot of the social and not-so-social drugs of the time, and my career faltered.

By now our home life was in serious need of repair, but I could not find the strength to keep things in order. The children were the ones who suffered most, changing from private to public schools and back again while I worried about myself. We did not give them any guidance and they faltered in their own lives. They needed an example from us of what a home should be, and we were not it. My children grew up in this confusion and moved out into the world to their own confusion. The example we set for them is their legacy.

Eventually one of Julia's boyfriends left his wife and children and moved to our city. He showed up at our door and was surprised to find we were a family. This caused real panic on the home front and forced Julia to confront her actions. Now she had to deal with the truth and found I would no longer look the other way. Ours became another falling-apart marriage, except that she had never married me, but the state, through common law, recognized our relationship as such.

Her solution was to move by herself to another state. This process took almost a year, as she would pack and have second thoughts and my blind love would let me think there was a chance. Finally I gave her a settlement, asked her to leave, and she moved for good.

After she left, my youngest son, who is now in his twenties, returned home, giving me a second chance with him.

I believed in marriage then, and I believe in it now. Whenever I brought it up, Julia always had an excuse but said, "If I ever get married, it will be to you." Our relationship was volatile, exciting, and filled with love, but it was never a loving and caring partnership. Her final departure was a wake-up call to get on with my life.

Paul

"You Have to Work on It"

Dear Reader,

When we married in 1960, I was nineteen and he was twenty-one and we loved each other madly. Even rereading this sentence makes me so light-headed I should probably lie down right now with a cold, wet cloth on my forehead. (Nineteen and twenty-one!) Our parents orchestrated a lovely formal reception and, smiling, walked us down the aisle. Today I would place my child in a locked facility if he or she attempted marriage at such a tender age. Anyway, we made a home for ourselves, worked, planned a future, developed friendships, and began raising a family. Also, we continued to love each other, even though he could be so stupid sometimes I'd have to yell at him. He worked eight days a week when his business was new, although I sarcastically observed I'd never seen an armored car following a hearse.

Sometime in the late sixties or maybe the early seventies, conventional wisdom decreed that in order to have a successful marriage, "You Have to Work on It." This was the exact phrase as it appeared in print and was voiced by numerous authorities on the subject of marriage. "You Have to Work on It" was the Rosetta stone of marital counsel. No discourse on marriage could be considered authentic until these magical words were intoned, whereupon listeners would nod their heads up and down and reply, "Oh, yes, of course."

A niggling worm of suspicion began to wriggle in my secret heart. Here I thought we were so compatible, contented, even passionate. I thought our marriage was terrific. Was I supposed to tinker around with the innards of our relationship the way a mechanic works on a carburetor? Perhaps I should be baking pies, arranging flowers, coloring my hair. What? Stupid me, I didn't have a clue.

Finally, bravely, I faced the problem. I asked him, "Are you consciously, deliberately 'working' on this marriage?" And do you know what he said? He said no, he didn't have a clue as to how *anybody* could even *begin* to work on a marriage, and besides, it sounded tedious. Like flossing your teeth or visiting your great-aunt Mildred.

After a while he learned to avoid the dumb moves that led to my raising my voice and slamming silverware around in the drawers and I discovered that if I took the time to explain my grievances, he, being a dear and considerate soul, would thereafter aim to please me.

Thirty-two years have slipped by, the children have grown up and left home (thank God), and we're back to just the two of us. We still don't have the slightest hint of where the marriage needs work. But what can you expect when two kids go off and get married?

Dorothy

"He was fighting for his life"

Dear Reader,

Two years ago we found out Bob had lymphoma. When I was first told, a thousand thoughts bounced around in my head. How would Bob handle this? How could I tell our daughters? Who could I turn to for advice? Which hospital? Which doctor? Not once did I allow myself to think too far into the future. I kept my questions to now, tomorrow, next week. I've always kept calm in a crisis. Okay, we have a problem. How can we solve it? What's next? I couldn't allow the ramifications of what I had just heard into my thoughts, not even a little. One step at a time.

Bob's reaction was what I expected. He'd been brought up by worriers. He broke down. His reaction was, "What I always feared has happened." I felt so helpless. I saw his pain. I wanted to make everything better. I said I understood, but I really didn't. I wondered how I would have reacted had it been me. I wanted him to be strong, to say, "We'll fight this together," just like in the movies.

Telling the girls was hard. Bob couldn't. It was up to me. They took it badly. I had to be strong so they could lean on me. I called on my stoic upbringing—keep your guard up, hold your feelings in. If I broke down, it would have been too much for them to bear.

Norma, a close friend who had intestinal cancer the year before, recommended books by Bernie Siegel and other positive thinkers and relaxation tapes. They helped me. They reaffirmed my belief in positive thinking, never allowing the inner thoughts, the negative ones, to surface. Bob tried but finally rejected this approach. Imagery, affirmations—I put notes all over the house. He laughed at me kindly and let me "do my thing." He even appreciated my efforts.

There were extra hugs and kisses, hand squeezing and holding, looks of love, sympathy, compassion. Not many words were exchanged. Was it that they weren't needed or that they couldn't be said? Bob took care of wills, insurance, stocks, and so forth. We talked about them matter-of-factly, never admitting why we were suddenly doing this.

Bob had a curable type of lymphoma. The odds were good. I maintained my positive outlook. He was hospitalized for his first treatment so his reactions could be monitored. Both girls were there. How important family is at these times! I still felt I had to keep up the facade, to play the role of martyr—everything will be all right. It was so hard to see the person I love, whom I've spent so much of my life with, helpless, weak, and frightened.

We received wonderful support from friends and family. The phone never stopped ringing. Bob spoke to everyone and cried each time. He seemed to like the attention. Did he enjoy the sympathy? The less I talked, the better I liked it. There was a point when I didn't want to answer the phone. I wanted to scream, "Enough! How many times can you talk about it? Why go over it again and again? Stop wallowing and get on with it!" I had to stop myself. He was fighting for his life. How dare I tell him how to do it?

There were two Bobs—the one I saw and the brave face he put on for everyone else. He'd leave for work (part time) feeling cranky and tired and impatient, only to appear at the office cheerful and brave. I'd get calls telling me how wonderfully he was accepting this awful thing. To me he was grumpy, sad, angry, at times unkind. We all have different faces for different places. I know that. But why couldn't he try on that happy face for me?

He underwent sixteen weeks of chemotherapy as an outpatient. Those days were awful. One of the medications Bob was taking didn't allow him to sleep, so I didn't sleep. He managed to make enough noise to wake me and keep me up. His pills were all over the house. He jumped and yelled if I moved them. I confided in our daughter, who urged us to join a support group. Bob refused. He couldn't face being with other cancer patients. Why couldn't I be understanding? He was the one who had this awful sickness. What was I so mad about?

Halfway into Bob's treatment, I had an accident. Coming out of a driveway, I misjudged the speed of an oncoming car. My car was totaled. A few inches more and I, too, would have been totaled. How did this happen? Too much on my mind, overworked, overtired, stressed out. In all the time of Bob's illness, and even to this day, only two people have asked how I was. People wait until Bob leaves the room and whisper, "How's he doing? He seems to be handling it so well." The accident was my way of saying, "Here I am, look at me, I need attention too." Fortunately, no one was hurt. I realized I couldn't go on like that. Bob and I talked and talked about me, the things I was holding inside. We both knew we needed help. We had to face our mortality. We began to see a therapist.

I found a support group for spouses and caregivers of cancer patients. Thank heaven for those wonderful people. It was a small group, some men, mostly women. We could honestly tell each other how we felt. I could finally be open about my feelings. I felt safe there.

The sixteen weeks of chemo finally ended and all of the tests came back okay. He gained weight and began to feel like himself again. Did we go back in time to where and who we were before this thing? No. He says cancer is always on his mind. Every time he goes for a checkup he becomes withdrawn, angry. I understand. Every ache and pain makes him think the cancer has returned.

Has he changed? Yes. So have I. His feelings about life are different, his sense of what's really important. I thought he'd take better care of himself. Instead he overeats. He loves good food but doesn't exercise. He spends more money than he should. Doesn't he care about me, about us? I'm tired of nagging. I've become more independent. Are we closer now? Sometimes I think so, sometimes I'm not sure. We still love each other, but this experience didn't deepen our love, which makes me sad.

How wonderfully romantic the storybook version is. In reality it doesn't happen that way.

Rose

"We were trapped together, and we could escape together"

My dear wife,

It hasn't always been easy. There were times I felt trapped. There was never a time, however, when I wanted to get out of the trap. They say love grows stronger when two people have shared trials and tribulations, and I agree. I love you more now than I did when we were twenty. I love you more because I know you better, and you know me more than I know myself. Our love is easy. I know I can go off the deep end and you won't leave me. You'll eventually point out my failings, but you won't leave. That's comforting. You've made our home a nice place to be, you've made our children nice people, and you've even made me nicer.

It eventually dawned on me that you were trapped as well. We were trapped together, and we could escape together. And we have. So I'm glad I'm trapped. I love you.

Your husband

❦

"Take a risk, break some rules"

Dear Reader,

One of the best lessons I learned about life and, indirectly, about marriage was from our two dogs. Our first was an overtrained poodle who never did anything wrong. We loved him dearly, but after a while he became boring. Our second was a daffy, dizzy shorthaired pointer. She was poorly trained, barked madly at everyone, and thought she was an equal member of the family. She ruined our carpets the first week we had her, stole our food, demanded attention, and nevertheless charmed all of us with her verve and high spirits. When she was chastised, she made sure we loved her by snuggling up until we patted her generously.

The lesson: It does not pay to be good, bland, and ultimately boring. Take a risk, break some rules, get the love you need by asking for it. This will keep a marriage frisky and charm the one who most needs charming.

Rita

"The minute you become involved, your life changes"

Dear Reader,

In 1980 in Tel Aviv, I had a fight with a South African friend. "You'll marry someone with an accent," she cursed. The next year, Federico Fellini's palm reader in New Delhi predicted, "You'll marry someone from a different part of the world."

Small wonder that when I finally met a man with all the wonderful qualities I'd been searching for, he turned out to be Russian.

I think we have a pretty terrific marriage. We love

each other. We care about each other. We're best friends. We're partners. He's my best fan (and the only one outside of my friend Suzanne who thinks I'm hysterically funny). He has dozens of endearing names for me. When we're apart, he telephones me constantly. But being married to a Russian isn't like being married to an American.

We met in Rome, where I was then living, in pre-glasnost 1985. I'd given up my apartment and was staying for a few months with friends who had an extra bedroom. They had a friend in California who had a Russian friend trying to get to Rome from Vienna in order to defect. Eventually he arrived, very dramatically, and somehow we became a couple almost immediately, although I was definitely not looking for a relationship at that moment. Nor had I ever before been attracted to blond, blue-eyed men.

The minute you become involved with anyone, your life changes. Becoming involved with a Russian who has just defected has lots of added dimension. Like paranoia. All of the Russians I know who grew up before Mikhail Gorbachev ushered in a new political era are paranoid in the extreme. It's something they never really get over.

KGB agents, spies, and betrayal are very Russian and definitely an aspect of my accented marriage. Before the fall of the Soviet Union in 1991, whenever Alexei met another former Soviet, he immediately sized him up, trying to discern if he, or she, ever belonged to the KGB. During our first years together, in the middle of the afternoon Alexei would draw the living room curtains so a Soviet visitor couldn't see that the house overlooks a ravine. He guarded every word he said over the telephone. Some of his messages, about ordinary domestic chores like making a bank deposit, were too cryptic to understand.

Sometimes the paranoia was justified. One day, maybe six months after we'd arrived in the United States, I got a call from a radio station in San Francisco. The caller, an American, said when Alexei was there giving an interview he'd left some materials they wanted to return. Without a thought, I gave them our address. When Alexei learned of the call, he flew into a rage because I'd been careless with information so precious. (This, despite the fact that our name is in the phone book.) He felt the caller was from the KGB, which was trying to track him down. Sure enough, a few days later the Soviet Consulate sent an unpleasant but very official letter, which Alexei fished out of the mailbox with salad tongs, fearing germ warfare. After a year's worth of calls to and from the FBI, the consulate stopped harassing us. By then glasnost was already happening.

When we first came here, Alexei's defection rated huge headlines, but he didn't immediately find work in his profession. His English wasn't good enough, he was confused about the huge step he'd taken, and he had terrible professional advice. It seemed to me he should wait on tables, drive a cab, do whatever people do to earn a living when they aren't working in their profession. He couldn't. In Russia you are what you are and there isn't much crossing over. It was only after a few years, when my boss disappeared without paying me, that Alexei volunteered to work for a Russian building contractor. I know he hated hammering and sawing and working for minimum wage. But he did it. I always thought that taking the job was a major step in his integration into this society. Whether he would do it again I don't know, because after that he finally began to work in his own profession.

There are only two differences our marriage couldn't survive, I think, and I'm lucky neither has become an issue. The first is religion. I'm not an observant Jew, but I spent eleven years in Israel. I am deeply attached to my heritage and emotional about my Jewish identity. I married Alexei knowing he wasn't a practicing Christian, but I worried during our first few years that he, who had grown up without religion, would suddenly discover the Russian Orthodox Church and become a devout follower. I never would have opposed this. It just would've made me extremely uncomfortable. Fortunately, Alexei seems quite happy spending the Jewish holidays with my family and, despite my urging, has steadfastly refused even to get a Christmas tree, which Russians call a New Year tree.

When I married Alexei, I married a man without a

family. At the time we met, his mother, father, and the aunt who helped raise him were still alive and in Moscow. He'd contemplated defecting for many years, knowing it would mean never seeing his family again. Then glasnost happened, and in October 1991 Alexei returned. By then his aunt and father had died. He saw his mother a few times and then she died as well. But seeing her again after so many years of separation was wonderful for him, as he rediscovered his original childhood feelings for her and felt close once more.

So my family has become his family. Fortunately, my parents and my husband all like one another, and they have a lot in common. Early on we had a rare fight, which ended with Alexei storming out of the house. I waited and waited for him to return. When he didn't, I got in the car and drove to my mother to be comforted, only to find that he was already there. That's when I knew for sure we were inextricably bound together and fated to have a long and enduring marriage.

Alexei just read this and wants to add that, like many Russians, he writes poetry. Even now, whenever he's depressed or faces overwhelming problems, he writes poetry. Words have helped him survive the darkest times of his life and his defection. I asked if he ever writes about me. He says I'll have to learn Russian to find out.

Jill

"After twenty-eight years, we're comfortable"

Dear Reader,

I love my husband and he loves me, but even love doesn't explain the longevity of our relationship. I've never thought of leaving him, but occasionally I've thought of boiling him in oil. To explain why our marriage has stayed healthy, I can't say what we do, but I'll tell you what we don't do.

We don't take each other seriously most of the time. When Mike comes home from a frustrating day, looks at the lawn, and growls, "See the grass. That gardener is an incompetent SOB. You talk to him," I just smile and say, "Okay, honey." I know he's really saying he had a rotten day and couldn't yell at the person he was mad at, so he's going to take it out on me. I don't fall into the trap of yelling back because if I did, a real fight would start. Likewise, when I rant and rave, "I have no life," he keeps calm. He listens patiently and doesn't take it personally because he knows I'm really saying I've reached my limit.

When I begin to think my problems are unique, I have a proven method of relieving my frustration. I have a Häagen-Dazs sundae with my best friend and tell her what a creep I married. She's a true friend. She listens, commiserates, and then forgets everything I said.

Mike and I laugh at the lack of spice in our love life. I don't mean it isn't satisfying, but I can't remember the last time he dragged me away from the stove to a motel with a vibrating bed. We don't get hurt when we say to each other the spirit is willing but the flesh is exhausted.

We don't fight about money, politics, or religion. We don't have any, we disagree, and I go to church and he doesn't.

We're not always together. He traveled a great deal when we were first married and I moaned that I missed him, but I developed my own life. Having my own life meant I had something interesting to talk about other than the family, which can get pretty boring.

We don't have different hobbies. We consciously find an activity we both like and try to do it as much as possible. It gives us a common escape.

I also don't get bent out of shape when he doesn't think I'm wonderful, which is very infrequently, of course.

We didn't consciously set out to avoid certain relationship pitfalls. God knows we weren't that smart, educated, or sensitive. We did have one very important ingredient: we liked each other and we were friends. It's the most important element in our marriage. We forget it sometimes and the results are disastrous.

We've gone through periods when we felt that life passed us by, but then we looked around. We've raised three children to adulthood, buried my parents, bought two houses and too many cars to count. We've had wonderful friends and awful enemies and we've survived. After twenty-eight years, we're comfortable. We know each other so well we can anticipate each other's actions. We no longer suffer from the "wind syndrome," which my dearest describes so delicately as the condition of not being able to belch for fear of offending. He tells me the thought of having to be on his best behavior all the time would terrify him.

Our marriage isn't perfect. It would be awful to have a perfect relationship. It would be difficult, if not devastating, to find fault and, God forbid, discover we're like everyone else. Then, when we fell out of our self-absorbed dreamland, we'd have so far to tumble.

This all leads to the final "we don't," which is we don't think about shoulds, coulds, or ifs. No matter how green the neighbor's grass, he probably has grubs under the lawn. We don't envy, we fertilize, occasionally weed, and even pesticize. The result is a sturdy relationship that doesn't consume all of our time and energy and grows with routine maintenance and occasional replanting.

Of course, now that I've made it sound so sensible, I'm sure he'll tell me tonight he's found a twenty-three-year-old aerobics instructor and they're running away to Key West.

Claire

"Thank you for staying with me"

Dear Marjory,

Seventeen years ago, also on the eve of the New Year, I wrote to you, during our separation, asking you to recommit yourself to me, as I wanted to recommit myself to you. And you did, and I did, and we recommitted ourselves to each other.

Now we face the dawn of our twenty-sixth year together. With a new calendar year fast approaching, I thought it appropriate to pull myself away from another hand of solitaire to write this note of apology and prayer. This epistle is one of thanks for what has come before and a plea for what may come in the future.

As to the apology, I ask that you continue to accept me for who I am—my warts and farts and foibles—and offer no more of an excuse than the fact that I know and recognize how hard it must be to live with me. I appreciate the whys of my often-outrageous behaviors and can honestly identify both their source and the reasons for their persistence. However, my long-ago arrival at this introspective rest stop hasn't (yet) allowed me to allow myself to venture on the road less traveled. I fear if I don't control everything today or limit the potentially controllable as much as possible, tomorrow's slings and arrows will get me.

Despite your love and encouragement and despite the praise and recognition of less significant others, I retain my perception of unworthiness and nonbetterness. I fear being like my father and suspect that reality and its consequences are just around the corner.

My job change occurred just as Meg was going to college and was weirdly reminiscent of my own experiences with my father. And the widening profile and increasing chins I see each day in the mirror serve to confirm that I'm continually becoming more like him. With a beard, I don't see me as him so clearly. Without it, it's "He's here again!" And when I'm told I sound like him and I hear it too . . . I don't want this.

Strangely, but in a way I'm not too sure about yet, his death has resulted in some perception that I've inherited whatever little energy he had left. It was out there somewhere and I've sorta sucked it up.

For all of this I'm sorry. I'm scared and angry about

the prospect of failing and so I exercise that fear and exorcise that anger inappropriately at the most convenient whipping girl. You're available all (or most) of the time to catch these eruptions and, for the most part, you're the safest person with whom to share my wrath. But, given who you are and what you do to continue to piss me off . . . Stop. This is supposed to be an apology.

I can't (won't) give up my fear of not succeeding, not yet. I can't let go of my need to control, yet. I can't overcome my obsession over not having enough means to pay for the future, even with the positive fiscal realities of the present staring me in my monthly brokerage account face. I want to be rich, but I haven't come to grips with the fact that I'll never be or with the fact that I possess great riches in you and Meg.

As to the prayer or plea for the future, I want things to move forward. The trauma and anxiety that we—and it was we—faced as you completed your doctorate brought out the best in us, or at least it brought it out more often than not. I want to replicate that effort and the pleasure it has brought.

While I'm most truly proud and sincerely appreciative of your monumental accomplishment, your success places me in a most difficult conundrum. With the passing of each summer, when the dissertation was finally going to be finished but wasn't, I was the winner. I retained another issue to give you shit about. As the

83

years dragged on, I knew I was better than you in something. Sure, everybody liked and respected you, but you couldn't finish this job.

But you actually did finish it, and it was good. And I'm basking in the reflected glow of your achievement and it makes me feel good about you and about me and about us. I'm so happy for you and pleased to see you receive kudos from everyone who loves and admires you. It's made me reexamine how I viewed you and how I perceived my role as husband/father/boss—rightly or wrongly. It will help me change and work on the two of us.

And tomorrow will be better. Please help me make it so.

Thank you for staying with me and loving me. Thank you for helping me change and become better and for resisting my efforts to change you. Thank you for adapting to my many ugly and annoying habits, and for adopting some of the few things I've been right about. And thank you for growing older with me in all the good ways.

I love you and will always do so.

Tim

Note: The following letter is written by Marjory, the wife of the contributor of the previous letter, to their daughter.

"We choose each other every day in small ways"

Dear Meg,

I just got back from our walk together and our good discussion (or call it loving argument) about your plans. Although I was honest, I haven't said all I want to say. I want to talk to you about life, love, and an enduring relationship with a man.

Your choice of mate will be the most personal, intimate, and significant life choice you'll make. I want you to benefit from my mistakes and from my learnings.

First the learnings. When I chose your father, both in 1967, when I married him, and in 1977, when we reunited after our two-year separation, there were rational factors in my decision. Call it reason, call it love, it doesn't matter. But these things were certain. I love to look at him. To me he's the most handsome man in the world—rugged yet refined features, warm, sensitive eyes, which make me melt, and soft, curly hair, which I'll remember when he goes completely bald. I knew when I met him I'd never tire of looking at him.

A second compelling attraction was his intellect. His awareness of the world around him, his broad knowledge of things political, cultural, and artistic, and his continuous love for reading and current events told me we'd never be at a loss for words. Even now, after twenty-five years together, we always have things to talk about. And I respect his intelligence, as do others around him.

Of course, your dad's wit and wacky sense of humor also exerted a strong magnetic pull. He's always made me laugh. And he's learned to temper the cynical and sarcastic parts of his humor so he's no longer hurtful.

The physical attraction that some people call chemistry has always been there with Dad, but not always to the same extent. Life's conditions exert an influence on chemistry. It's hard to find him sexy when I'm angry. It's hard to feel sexually appealing when I'm not feeling good about myself. But I believe this ebb and flow in the physical relationship between two people is natural. It's not possible to maintain the same level of intensity in an intimate relationship that is embedded in day-to-day living.

From the beginning, and reinforced over time, I've known Dad to be a good man, sensitive, loving, full of integrity, practical, and loyal. I know you'll agree he's been a great father, something difficult for him given his own family history. These are attributes I value and some of the reasons we've stayed together for twenty-five years.

Mistakes I've made are things you know about, because you were there. You lived through some of the terrible fights. You heard us bicker and nitpick. You saw me let Dad get away with saying things that hurt me, and you saw me let my resentment build up over time. You even met some of the men I spent time with during the separation, although I don't think you got to know any of them.

I learned something important during the separation. There are lots of men I could love—some who are intelligent, others with whom there's chemistry. And I know I could have made a life together with someone other than your father. That life wouldn't have been the same, it might have been easier, but I still would have had to work at it.

Life with your dad hasn't always been easy, but it's been fun, and full, and most wonderful because of the joy you bring us. But it wasn't fate that brought us together. I chose him and he chose me. And we chose each other again, after some tough times. We choose each other every day in small ways, like when he calls me in the middle of the day to tell me about a nice phone call he got from a client or when he helps me with some jam I've gotten myself into. I choose him when I remember to check before making a social engagement or make a conscious effort not to suggest eating out when he's worried about money.

In the past we chose with our hearts and with our heads. Living together day to day means choosing with our actions.

I wish you good fortune, strength, courage, and the ability to take risks, so you too may choose with your heart and your head. Once you make a choice, I know your actions will make it true and make it work.

Mom

"Remember that passion is not love"

Dear Daughter,

Cupid's arrow is dipped in passion. Once shot, his arrow is difficult to evade. It penetrates the strongest barriers and spurns its only antidote, which is reason. Passion is a demon in the calculus of marriage. You cannot do without it since love unfolds from passion's chrysalis. Yet passion so clouds reality that, alone, it cannot sustain a marriage.

If you conclude that I believe marriage is largely a matter of luck, you are right. No matter what advice is provided, no matter what admonitions offered, once passion shapes your decision, it is hard to turn back. But passion does not last. Like a shooting star, passion will burn out, hopefully later rather than sooner.

Before the fire diminishes, love must flower and companionship be cultivated if a marriage is to have any chance of success. By love I mean the unrestrained desire to share, and by companionship I refer to an ease of being together. If you share what you now covet for yourself, you enhance the possibility of success. You must be willing to surrender part of yourself and become open, so emotionally transparent that your mate can read your inner thoughts. I can express these words glibly, but the conditions are difficult to achieve. The commitment in marriage is of a high order.

You are existentially selfish. I do not say this in a deprecating way. You were raised to be special, and you are. Yet I now suggest that you relinquish part of your individuality, part of what makes you special, for your anticipated marriage. This would be an extraordinary act of generosity and the single most important display of your love.

This does not mean you must always sacrifice for your mate. In fact, slavishness undermines a relationship. But you must be prepared to sacrifice, and occasionally do so.

On life's many highways you may take a route not in total harmony with the wishes of your spouse. Without sacrificing your marital vows, you will have to find a way to retain your individual goals. This will be difficult, but weigh your sense of personal fulfillment against the pleasures of marriage, and approach your spouse willing to give. By the way, demand nothing less from him.

Your mother and I could not give, most certainly not

in the way the other needed. Our divorce was nonetheless painful. If you are not sure about your ability to give, or suspect that your mate cannot give up some part of his self for your relationship, do not marry. A person does not evolve into someone different from who he is.

Remember that passion is not love, love is a necessary but insufficient condition for successful marriage, and successful marriage is most of all a function of sharing, generosity, and moderating selfish impulses. Surely you will do well. Yet if all else fails, pray. It may not guarantee success, but it will not hurt. I love you.

Dad

"What has kept us together are the qualities we share"

Dear Reader,

It has not been easy to write this. Words and thoughts collide midbrain as I struggle for order and clarity in my feelings about marriage. Marriage is a great crap shoot, and despite my difficulties in getting it right, I would not give up trying to make it work. After the romance and passion, the courting and the mating games, there is a lot of adjusting to living with a stranger "till death do us part." Most of us are so inadequately prepared for what this entails.

I was brought up to be self-reliant, honest, virtuous. According to my father, happiness was a by-product of hard work. Growing up, I always strove to please. Life was not "sexy." Affection was more implicit than explicit. My family members never shared their feelings about one another. I felt secure, however, thought I was happy, and assumed with equanimity that my married life would be a continuation of that condition.

It was not. My first marriage ended in divorce. On the surface, we should have been compatible, we shared so many interests. Lacking was the ability to communicate easily and openly on anything pertaining to the relationship. We simply could not trust ourselves to trust each other.

Second time around, I am still learning how to love, to give love, to accept it as it is given; to weave and duck when anger comes at me and deal with issues when the anger subsides; to rebut what is unfair and learn from what is valid criticism.

I have dealt with the tough times first. However, we do have fun and happiness and good times. The kindness and generosity shown to me and my family are deeply appreciated. I feel I have grown wiser and stronger by resolving, rather than running away from, my problems.

What has kept us together are the qualities we share and hold dear: honesty, generosity, the ability to share confidences, and good humor (without which no relationship can survive). This time around there is trust, and two stubborn people are learning how to make a good marriage a happy one.

Kitty

"I am so proud you are my Wifey"

Dear Wifey,

It is nearly five years since our wedding. In these five years, you have made me happier every day. Every day since then, I have loved you more. Every day I thank you for begging and insisting we get married.

You have given us the joy of Matthew and Franny. You directed our move to our beautiful new home and made our lives so natural, fulfilling, and elegant, that it seems we have always been here.

In the last five years, our pleasures have been great because of you. You are constantly cheerful, forgiving, patient, loving, loyal, and thoughtful. Most of this is demonstrated daily when you listen to me snore at night.

While the loss of your father was nearly impossible

for us to bear, you have lived your life hereafter as a loving benediction to him. He lives on in you, Matthew, and Franny.

So this is my testament of appreciation to you. You have grown every year in the last five, while managing to lose five pounds. You work, play, mother, housekeep, cook, psychoanalyze, motivate, decorate, and enrich every day. It is impossible to imagine not being married to you. I know my life would never be the same. Besides, I would be lost, hungry, and disorganized.

Please accept this letter as my Christmas present to you for this year. I love you with all my heart. Besides, I spent all my money on the sound system, so this is it.

It is impossible to imagine anyone better than you. But somehow you will still improve over the next five years. I love you. I adore you. I am so proud you are my Wifey. Thank you.

John

"All any of us really wants is to feel understood"

Dear Reader,

I've thought a lot about my two marriages. I feel I learned a lot from both of them and I'll be able to enter the next relationship enriched and much, much wiser about how good relationships work.

I was twenty-one years old, had graduated college, gone to Europe, driven across America, had affairs, smoked dope, worked for civil rights, and protested the Vietnam War. What else was there to do but get married?

I do believe I'd have married Attila the Hun had he crossed my path at that moment, but instead I married Kevin, just off the plane from a year's stint in Vietnam as a medic. What did either of us know about post-traumatic stress disorder? We tried hard to make the marriage work. He went to therapy, we moved across the country to Portland, we both went to therapy, marriage counseling. We even tried to have a baby. Throughout our marriage, I supported Kevin while he tried to find work. In Portland I supported us for four years while he went to college. Then we moved back across the country, but nothing helped and I was still supporting Kevin, so I left him in Brooklyn Heights. We'd learned from our various therapies how to live together, and I suppose we could have lived together for the next fifty years. But we both knew we couldn't seem to help each other grow, and I didn't want to support him anymore.

I think a small vignette from our time together will illustrate some of what went wrong. We lived together before we got married. Kevin ironed his shirts and I took out the garbage, and we were happy. Then two weeks after we were married, he was yelling at me because his shirts weren't ironed, and I was yelling at him to take out the damned garbage. Somehow we couldn't be who we were because now we were *married*, and *married* people did things one way while single people did them another. It was many years before I fully understood how powerful these preconceived notions of marriage are, and what damage they did to what was initially a relationship with possibilities.

There was another powerful force at work inside me, one I really didn't understand until I found myself married for the second time, only to discover I'd married a part of Kevin all over again.

Between marriages, I had seven years of single life in which I was very happy. I dated, had affairs, and did pretty much as I pleased. I traveled a great deal and finished my master's and began my doctorate. And, as they say, it was good.

Just when I wasn't looking, I fell in love. As in madly, deeply, passionately, crazy in love. And even as I was falling, I remember saying to my good friend Angela, "If I get five good years out of this, I'll be happy." And I continued to fall.

Neal was nine years younger, from another country, another culture, another race, and yet when we were together it felt like that's how it always was. My mother said, "He's a dreamer." There were other warning signs but I was too giddy to pay attention. I found myself pregnant and we both knew we wanted this baby, so a month before Mathias was born, we got married. Marriage wasn't something I wanted to do again, and Neal really didn't care either way, but we felt this child would face enough prejudice in the world, so we married.

The first few years were really wonderful, but then that funny thing began to happen again. My dreamer couldn't seem to get his life together to support us, so I went back to work and became the main support. He really wanted a second child, and I was very reluctant by this time because the marriage had become frayed and cracked around the edges, but I was still very much in love with him and didn't want another divorce, so I had another baby, Sam. While I was pregnant I learned that Neal had been having an affair. After the birth, which was pretty traumatic, I had to go back to work full time because he'd run up thousands and thousands of dollars of debt on my credit cards. When Sam was only five months old and Mathias was six, I divorced Neal. It's been five years since that terrible time of disappointment, hurt, and rage, and I feel pretty much healed. I keep thinking to myself, *There's a message, here, Sue. You've done this twice. Let's not go for three strikes.*

Well, there is a message and I believe I finally get it. I think I'm not alone in this, either. There's always been a dreamer inside me, but I was raised a good Italian Catholic girl who really learned how to be responsible. I didn't feel I could be a dreamer, so I married dreamers, thinking they'd release the dreamer in me and we could float off together. It never occurred to me that someone has to support a dreamer. I poured everything I had into these men and their dreams, thinking that by doing this, their dreams would become reality and then they'd help me float my dreams. I didn't see that what they really wanted was simply to dream and dream and dream. Reality wasn't their goal.

Now I finally understand (it only took forty-eight years) that I need to nurture the dreamer in me. I must choose to be responsible first to the dreamer in me, and then I can continue to dream. I must choose a man who has made his dreams real himself and who continues to dream. Then we would have a marriage made in heaven.

A few final random thoughts and observations. What seems to cause the most trouble in relationships is unspoken expectations. You know the ones I mean: Well, I thought once we were married you would . . . And then there are always sexual expectations. They get voiced only in front of other people, as jokes. What seems to work the best is the ability to really listen and weigh another's words, not judging them out loud. And having a sense of humor is key. All any of us really wants, I believe, is to feel understood and accepted.

Sue

"I've learned a new technique: hostility management"

Dear Reader,

I'd like tell you something about being married to Fred. To do this I need to begin by telling you about Fred. He's nurturing, companionable, sweet, funny, intelligent, sensitive, ethical, uncomplicated, and—above all—I love the way he uses words.

Here are some other things you probably should know about Fred. He can be withdrawn, silent, moody, and uncommunicative. There are times when I wonder if he remembers how to talk. One of Fred's basic philosophical tenets seems to be "a feeling verbalized is a feeling demeaned." He also appears to have an insatiable appetite for TV sports.

Fred is a great father.

Fred is the human embodiment of the still waters that run deep.

I really like being married to Fred. Like every Friday night when he comes home with a bouquet of flowers. Or when I'm tired and he knows my back needs rubbing and—without even being asked—he goes directly to the exact source of pain. Or when he knows the right thing to say to help me put my work problems in perspective. Sometimes I tell Fred he lives inside my head, because it's uncanny how well he understands exactly what's going on there. And most of the time his understanding of me is accompanied by generous dollops of support. For example, he gave up a job he loved so I could pursue my career more readily.

I could go on and on about the things he does just to make me feel happy and loved. As corny as it sounds, there are moments when I'm so overwhelmed by Fred's inner beauty and the life we share together that tears of joy flow. My kids say I'm a sentimental slob and laugh at me. But in those moments I feel incredibly blessed.

But there are also times when I feel incredibly frustrated. Let me try, through an example, to describe the Feelings of Frustration with Fred syndrome.

This past year I've reconnected with the Jewish part of me after a thirty-year hiatus from any kind of religious or spiritual commitment. Fred, although ethnically Jewish, was raised in a totally assimilated environment. He learned virtually nothing about Judaism as a child. He has had absolutely no contact with it as an adult. Nevertheless, he reacted with hostility when I first began my meager and tentative testing of the Jewish waters. Here's what he did: when he knew I was engaged in any of my Jewish activities, he became monosyllabic and turned cold.

I've tried to understand why he acts this way. As best I can ferret out, he thinks an attachment to Judaism on my part will create a divide between us. We'll no longer be able to connect with our accustomed closeness.

You know, of course, all about self-fulfilling prophesies. But what I'm trying to describe is something more akin to an inexorable tide that seems at times to sweep us both into a deep and forbidding whirlpool.

The truth is, I no longer share some of the things that are really important to me with Fred. So I can avoid his hostility, I seldom tell him when I'm meeting with my study group partners or about the things I'm learning that are adding new and wonderful dimensions to my life. What's the point?

In short, I've learned a new technique for marital happiness: hostility management. I simply withhold information that's going to produce hostility. I don't feel guilty. I certainly don't feel dishonest. What I do feel is sad that I've been forced to hide a part of me from someone with whom I'm deeply committed to sharing my life.

I've tried to counter this sadness with a philosophical outlook. No marriage is perfect. Certainly I'm not perfect. It's not reasonable to expect the man I love to be perfect. Given a choice between focusing on his flaws or his strengths, I go for those parts of Fred that are a never-ending source of joy and comfort.

Roxanna

Note: *This contributor wrote to us six months later and added the following thoughts.*

Six months have passed since I first wrote. Today is the day after the Passover seder, an event Fred and I attended together. Fred was gracious. And despite the misgivings he had before we went, he had a good time. In this season of miracles, I experienced nothing short of the supernatural in my own household.

This morning, with spring displaying the first signs of its impending arrival, Fred decided to dewinterize his trench coat. His comment: "I've taken the inner lining out of my coat in the same way I've taken my inner self out of the closet."

What's happening? Where are we going and, even more important, where will this journey take us?

I don't know, but there's no doubt that the train has already left the station. In the last month Fred has attended two lectures at the temple, has gone to services once, and has offered to go on two other Friday nights. He's also done some reading on Jewish themes and encouraged me to visit Israel.

You ask, How did this get started? I'll tell you. I don't know, but it's a tradition. What I mean is, we both appear to be drawing on the tradition of partnership, friendship, and closeness developed over the course of our twenty-five-year marriage. This tradition impels us to share and heal any breaches. Fred has figured out that we can be closer if he tries to understand what I'm doing. Conversely, we'll be farther apart if he tries to change me through hostility.

Query: Was I practicing self-delusion by choosing to interact only with the engaging side of Fred? Or did my strategy of less-than-full disclosure reflect some incredible maturity? Maybe this willingness to adapt my behavior to Fred's quirks shows I've achieved total acceptance of the real Fred, a man who has both beauty marks and warts. After all, why wave a red flag in front of a bull? If there are things I do that make Fred feel uncomfortable, why share them?

But this begs the question. I preferred to withhold a part of me from Fred so I wouldn't become uncomfortable when he exhibited gestures of discomfiture.

In a way, what I've shared with you is a love story. It's about two people who find ways to grow together rather than apart even when the change that such growth implies is threatening. Truly my cup runneth over!

"A common study is a great bonding force"

Dear Reader,

Perhaps it is not surprising that in many areas my wife and I lead quite separate lives because each of us has different interests and skills. For example, she is a great painter and craftsman. I need help holding a brush. However, it may be more of a surprise how close our lives have become in other areas, how our interests and involvement intersect in ways they didn't and couldn't two decades ago, when we were first married.

An obvious area of intersection is the family, and certainly deeply involved as we are in the lives of our teenage children, our lives converge in this area. Probably less obvious an area of growing intersection over these years has been in matters of faith. Normally a very personal thing not much discussed even with close friends, we have found ourselves engaged in an ever growing dialogue about what we believe and why. The dialogue began in a modest way about fifteen years ago and has grown year by year to the point where now these discussions are a regular part of our life together.

We share readings, we test ideas, we share discussions we have had with others. For some couples I think faith is a dividing line—each attend separate institutions, or one doesn't attend at all, children go to one parent's institution and know little about the other's. This separateness can be a source of division that may be great or small depending on how seriously one spouse takes the commitment and how much the other spouse resents the demands of this commitment.

I must say, parenthetically, that I have particularly admired those couples in which one partner, though not so inclined by nature or disposition, has made a very conscious effort to understand and be a part of the faith that is a significant aspect of the other spouse's life. This is especially admirable where the effort has been made across major religious or denominational lines. I can think of a handful of couples for whom I know this to be the case, and I think it speaks very well of their marriages and of the strength of their love for each other. It is also my impression that the results have been quite positive in that the spouse who is the recipient of this attention understands and appreciates the commitment involved and the love that commitment reflects. It is a real strengthener for the marriage.

For us, the shared interest grew following the death of my father and the baptism of our firstborn, a son, both of which occurred in the same year. My wife and I come from liturgically different denominations within the broad Protestant tradition. While these denominations are not very far apart theologically, our own views on matters of faith were really quite different and, frankly, when we started out, not particularly well informed.

We were fortunate to have a clergyperson who, by example more than preaching or teaching, led us into a much deeper desire to understand our faith and opened us to probing it in depth. The experience started modestly, with us involved more in the administrative side than the theological. Over time the emphasis changed. For a while our ideas and beliefs grew farther apart. Then, as we spoke more and exchanged materials, information, and perspective with a real desire to understand what the other was saying and with a profound respect for the intellect and study that went into each other's positions, we found our thoughts converging more and more.

Ironically, as our thoughts converged, the doctrinal differences—never fully resolved and perhaps not resolvable—receded in importance. What remained was the strength of a shared faith, the essentials newly rediscovered in their simplicity and a higher level of understanding of what the simplicity is all about.

For the purposes of this letter, the specifics of the resolution are less significant than the process. The fact that the process consists of regular dialogue on this subject is a strengthener of major significance for our marriage. In a world where many forces tear at relationships, a common study of significance to both our lives is a great bonding force.

My recommendation: find an area of intensely shared interest and build on it together. In lives that must necessarily be separate in so many ways, let this be a unifying bond and source of shared joy in, and appreciation of, each other.

Christopher

"Why don't more couples work together?"

To: My Spouse, President
From: Your Spouse, Managing Partner
RE: We just don't spend enough time together.

Memos aren't something husbands and wives should be writing to each other. A succinct love letter stuck on the bathroom mirror, maybe. A red rose on a pillow, perhaps. But since we're in business together, I thought I'd do some reflecting about our decision three years ago to head out into the business world as a team.

You can't argue with why we wanted to do this. We worked in related fields, business for both of us was stagnant, our first child had just turned one and we wanted another. Getting out of the city was a priority as well as having a work life that didn't resemble that of our respective parents.

To say our little endeavor has been a success is to call a grand slam a base hit. To date we've accomplished most of our agenda: enjoy "working the business," increase business, spend more time with the children, and, of course, remain happily married. There is, however, one goal we haven't achieved, and it may sound bizarre: we just don't spend enough time together.

Sure, we're together a lot. But all our time together is with others: our children, our clients, our staff, our parents, and our friends. Sometimes out of the blue I ask you the seemingly inane question "Honey, where did you go to high school?" You always look at me like I'm crazy. What I'm trying to say is that I want some time alone with you. Time alone so we can talk about what we want to talk about. Not what our clients or children or parents want to discuss.

If we got a new customer every time I've been asked, "How can you stand working with your spouse? Don't you get sick of each other?" we'd be rivaling AT&T in profits. My answer has always been to answer with a question: "Why don't more couples work together?" I guess they just don't know what it's like to be with someone like you.

❧

"We made the right decision at the outset"

Dear Reader,

My wife proposed to me one evening at a hamburger place on Columbus Avenue in Manhattan. I don't recall its name, but I still remember it. The place was stylish, the burgers were great, the service was indifferent, and the proprietor was surly.

I always said I wouldn't mind marrying someone, as long as I didn't have to live with her. That's pretty much the way it worked out for a while. I'm a newspaper reporter, and before we got married (I was twenty-eight, she was a year younger), I was told I would be sent to Tokyo as a foreign correspondent. We had separate apartments in New York, and since I was soon taking off for Japan, there was no sense in moving in together. After a one-week honeymoon we went back to our respective apartments, just like before.

I went to Japan alone, which would be the pattern for the next nine years in three postings abroad—Tokyo, Manila, and London. My wife, a freelance writer, would go, but late, kicking and screaming, and then not want to leave once ensconced in the new place. A reasonable approach on her part, but as we both knew, it was a ritual show of resistance, lobbying for sympathy (unlikely) and benefits (a sure thing, up to a point).

The exception was Manila. She stayed in Tokyo. Again, a reasonable decision, because Tokyo was a much better place for someone writing about the things she did, mostly culture and features. She came down to visit me every month or so and do stories from there or wherever I was off to—Australia, New Zealand, Hong Kong, Taiwan. During the winter months I tried to make it to Tokyo. The tiny apartment she moved into was like an ice cube in the winter, so the additional body heat was welcome on cold nights.

We once figured out that during the first four years we were married, we lived together only about half the time. A friend, explaining why his first marriage broke up, said, "It's not the years, it's the miles."

Maybe, but it worked out just the opposite in our marriage. The time spent apart was no big deal because I never thought our marriage was some fragile thing that needed constant tending to stay alive. We made the right decision at the outset, and a year or two spent apart wasn't going to change that. Besides, the separations do have their advantages. If you haven't seen someone for a few weeks, the reunions have a certain edge that coming home from a day's work doesn't.

And we have seen the world together, dozens

of countries, from north of the Arctic Circle in Scandinavia to the antipodes of Australia and New Zealand. In Japan we suffered through language lessons together, two mornings a week at dawn, and a summer vacation spent in a language boot camp. In Moscow, when the Stalin-era hotel where we were booked gave us a room but no seats at the restaurant, we foraged for food together.

Outside Zamboanga, in the southern Philippines, we stayed in a place where the lizards climbing the walls were a godsend—they ate the bugs—and sounds of cicadas mixed with the crackle of M-16 fire in the distance as the communist guerrillas traded rounds with the military. Near Roveniemi, Finland, we stepped out from a sauna at midnight in June into what looked like late afternoon light, amazed by the fact of the phrase "Land of the midnight sun."

Someone once said that life is just the sum total of your experiences. Well, my wife and I have had plenty of adventures—the good, the bad, and the ugly, but mostly we had them together. My wife and I were good friends when we were married, and we're even better friends now. We've been married for nearly thirteen years, and I can honestly say I have never once regretted it.

Riley

❦

"Marriage would be easier if one had a guidebook"

Dear Reader,

It occurs to me that marriage, like traveling, would be easier if one had a guidebook as well as a good companion. Since neither Michelin nor Baedeker publishes a guide to marriage, as an experienced traveler I offer a few tips for the journey.

- Choose a mate who's physically and emotionally appealing. You don't want to wake up one morning to find you've been sleeping with the ugly grumpling.
- Memory lapses can be a boon to a happy marriage. You can't hold a grudge if you can't remember the problem.
- Training in the diplomatic corps would be useful, but if you can't afford to spend a year abroad, read how our founding fathers compromised to create the Constitution.
- Sign up for a Berlitz course, the language of the opposite sex. You can't communicate if you don't share a common tongue.
- Find common interests (for example, if he likes history and she likes shopping, buy shoes at Gettysburg!).

- Maintain your sense of humor. This will enable you to retain your perspective and ignore the wrinkles, potbellies, balding heads, and in-laws.

If you follow these tips and travel with an amiable partner, you're not apt to lose your way. Bear in mind, though, that there are dips in the road, occasional detours, and patches of ice to confront every traveler.

Patti

"Ken would have taken care of his Barbie"

Dear Reader,

My marriage hardly started on strong footings. Neither set of my grandparents had marriages that survived and my parents had a crummy marriage. Mom and Dad never raised their voices at each other. In fact, they never developed voices.

And somehow, marriage was always on my mind.

At age eight I convinced my father to buy me Barbie and her wedding dress. The beautifully detailed full-length lace dress cost more than the doll, a fact that my father repeated for days. I detected boasting in his speech about this dress that cost more than the doll. I guessed I'd done something right.

I put away my baby dolls and started my relationship with Barbie. She was either in her bathing suit or I was painstakingly dressing her for marriage. Weeks into the relationship, my mother announced that the doll needed street clothes. Thank God for my mother. She was always so practical.

My parents' marriage continued in a blur of nonexistence, but I had Barbie, and what I didn't see with my parents I could pretend with Barbie. Eventually Barbie got the stewardess outfit and Ken. Upon their engagement, she gave up her flight attendant job. In fact, my recollection is that she met Ken on her first flight. After their wedding, Barbie made drapes, shopped, and kept house. Ken came directly home after work to be with her. The newlyweds giggled when Barbie's garlic bread burned or the recipe from *Sunset* magazine didn't work— giggle giggle happy happy. Ken adored Barbie.

At thirteen I put Barbie and Ken away. At thirty I married, and I didn't wear a dress like Barbie's.

We married in a backyard with a smattering of family members and friends. (Barbie and Ken had a lavish wedding at the Beverly Hills Hotel.) Six weeks later I was pregnant. (Barbie never got pregnant. I put the dolls away before I even understood consummation.)

113

The day after our son was born, my husband was stricken with a stomach virus that was screaming through the city. Our baby was jaundiced, my vagina was cut and hopefully sewn up correctly, I was afraid to take a shit, and my husband was all consumed with his discomfort. (Ken would never have done this. Ken would have stiffened up and taken care of his Barbie.)

The three of us lived in the prettiest six-hundred-square-foot duplex with choo-choo train drapes in our son's room. My husband thought the place was hideous, and before our son was walking we were moved to a crumbling adobe fixer-upper. The roof leaked, electricity was in only two rooms, there was no heat, and I found dead mice in the oven. (Ken would never have considered asking his Barbie to live in that slum. Never, not even if the resale value would triple.)

Then there were the trips—his trips—to South America and later to Indonesia. He said it would be too hard for our son and me to make the trips. He was going to do a lot of heavy trekking and he really needed this meditative time to himself. Why couldn't I understand? (Why? Because Ken would never have gone without Barbie. Ken would have bought a time-share condo in Hawaii.)

My husband's career is the type that takes years to develop, hence financial struggles were part of the development process. There were times when my business provided the only funds and I wanted awfully bad for him to do something about it. (My Ken stayed at the same firm forever, never risking a month without a paycheck. Ken would never have let his Barbie pay the mortgage. Her money was for clothes and stuff.)

Last year I shipped the box containing Barbie and Ken from my mother's garage to my home. I waited until my son was playing tennis and my husband cruising on his Harley (need I even mention that Ken would never have bought a Harley) before I opened the box. Barbie's Desmond shoebox closet was filled with neatly arranged clothing. I removed the hanger from her stewardess outfit and smiled as I imagined removing the airline emblems and updating it to a 1990 power suit.

I opened the Mattel-made closet for Ken and was surprised to see more of Barbie's clothes hanging in there. Imagine. She had her clothes in there for more than twenty-eight years. (Ken obviously had never complained the way my husband does about my clothes on his side of the closet.)

Barbie and Ken stood like two mummies, meticulously wrapped. I removed the fabric and gently examined Barbie. She had on her ice blue velvet cigarette pants with a fuzzy V-neck sweater that had fallen off a shoulder, exposing her pointy, nippleless breast. I made a mental note that padded shoulders would be necessary in her power suit to offset those breasts. She looked exactly the same and somehow not attractive to me.

Ken tumbled out of his twenty-eight-year sleeping arrangement having lost some hair. I was shocked. Ken had aged. Having held that stiff position I'd put him in had taken a toll. He was hardly recognizable. I don't remember ever noticing the vacant stare and strained expression he was wearing. I can't believe he had that look on him before. He looked exhausted.

I held Ken close as I gently stroked his bald spot and rocked him. (Barbie never would have done this.)

Eileen

"I had a great need for others to approve of my husband"

Dear Reader,

My thoughts about my marriage are contradictory and inconclusive. It was difficult for me to decide whether or not to marry. The thought that perhaps someone else would be better suited nagged at me until my wedding day. I was amazed that my husband-to-be was sure of what he was doing, and my trust in his confidence carried me along. Strangely, a wonderful feeling of relief came over me once we were married. That's not to say I never again thought of marrying someone else, but I no longer felt panicky or confused.

A feeling of security and commitment began to pervade. Nonetheless, memories of previous boyfriends came to mind. Though I would think things through and ultimately reconfirm my choice for marriage, these recurring memories would leave me feeling a bit lost for the moment. It was as if I wanted the boyfriends waiting on the sidelines . . . just in case.

Although it's hard to admit, I had a great need for others to approve of my husband. I craved reassurance that they all perceived him as special. I had a mental list of expectations regarding social behavior, style of living, attitudes, and opinions, and I practically exploded with panic if he didn't conform to what I considered perfect behavior. I would find a way to let him know, each and every time, that he was not who I wanted him to be.

This was probably never apparent to others because I became expert at concealing my feelings and reactions. Even though I'm a person with close, important friendships, and I love to share my thoughts with friends, I'm careful when it comes to revealing my feelings about my husband and our relationship.

The need for approval from close family members remained intense, but I did calm down with friends. My need for my husband to behave perfectly resulted in the two of us having many discussions and arguments.

Magically, my confidence in the relationship began to build. I became a much better friend and gave him my support. I saw that his love, friendship, support, and trust had become integral to my being, and I didn't want to lose them.

I often look around at other couples to compare relationships. Are they happier? Do they love each other more? How do they interact? I've learned that I can never tell what is really going on, but when I do admire another relationship, I try to emulate and incorporate the essence of what I admire into my own.

In the privacy of my own thoughts, there will always be unsettling issues. It helps to remind myself of the strengths my marriage brings to me, independently, and to us, as a couple, and I treasure it. I realize I've come a long way.

Brenda

"My children think I'm lonely, but I'm not"

Dear Reader,

My son doesn't think my marriage is functional. He says his marriage is real and mine isn't and sometimes he thinks I'm nuts. But my marriage is functional for my husband and me and we're happy with it. In my opinion, a functional marriage is a marriage that works for the two people involved.

My husband has his own business and travels quite a bit on his own because his time is more flexible than mine. I work for a publisher. Often I don't see him for weeks at a time. My children think I'm lonely because I'm alone, but I'm not. When he's gone, I can relax and not have to worry about taking care of him, which I love to do. I kick off my shoes and I'm not on a house schedule. It's time just for me. I come home, eat when I want, read in bed, and watch old movies (which I love and he hates). I can just be lazy.

There are couples who feel that being married means always being together, doing things together, having the same friends, and sharing the same ideas. This is great if it works for them. My husband and I are both very independent in our likes and dislikes. We often disagree on issues or vacations and even friends. Our friends consist of his, mine, and ours.

We give each other lots of breathing space. He's always encouraged me to be my own person, and he's my confidant, my best friend, lover, and the most honest and intelligent person I know. We go on trips together, just the two of us, to get to know each other all over again, and catch up on each other's lives. We always learn something new about each other.

Do we have a real marriage? Is it a functional marriage? Some of my friends don't think so. They think he may have something going on the side. Well, they can think what they want. I know better, much better!

Roz

"I was determined never to become a bitchy wife"

Dear Reader,

When I married at the age of twenty-nine, I was determined never to become a bitchy wife who harps at, picks at, and complains to her husband. Through years of observing the relationships of married friends, neighbors, and relatives, I was bothered by the bitching I observed.

I'm not sure at what point in our early married life hints of these unpleasant behaviors sneaked out. I'd never before, in any relationship, behaved this way and couldn't understand why I'd begun. Was it because I was married? Could it have been the familiarity of the relationship? I was determined to set some guidelines for myself, and I really believe they've helped.

I treat my husband the way I want him to treat me. I'm polite when I make requests. I don't order him around. Small courtesies, little favors, treats, and surprises work well for us. I fix his favorite meal, offer a drink, write a card, or hide a note. These gestures don't take much time yet he feels special and loved.

I choose my battles instead of constantly having little squabbles. This helps me stop, think, and decide whether to make a big deal out of something. It's easy to lash out, blurting curt answers or accusations I regret within seconds, but my arguments make more sense when I don't react emotionally. Rather than antagonizing him, I try to think before I speak. Sometimes both of us are willing to be flexible, sometimes one of us gives in.

Our relationship with each other is our number-one priority. We have a wonderfully happy marriage and loving partnership. We consider each other's feelings and preferences in our decisions and we've learned to value each other as much as we did when we were dating. We go out, just the two of us, and arrange private time together, away from our children and work.

Children grow up and leave, jobs are completed, retirement comes, but relationships endure if they've been nurtured and not ignored.

Deirdre

"All of us nurtured by the marriage grow"

Dear Reader,

He often asked, "Do you feel married?" for several years after the ceremony seven years ago, but not so often in the past two years. He was asking whether my sense of relative certainty about being part of a couple in middle age—I am in the middle period of a second marriage—was beginning to feel anything like the married state of my twenties. The question assumes that the earlier and more carefree state of mind is recoverable and desirable. I guess I shared that assumption and had been nursing the wounds of disillusionment for nearly a decade. I really had thought I was mating for life at age twenty-one: "When I was young, oh so much younger than today . . ."

Fortunately that optimism continued long enough for a child to be conceived; by the time of the second marriage, my traveling companion was nine years old. When mother and son set out on this second marital journey, we two had been relocated in a new community for five years—he a fourth grader, I well along in a completely new career.

This second marriage immediately created a new family out of five people, ages four, seven, nine, forty-one, and forty-one. The family was like a new garden, not grown from seed but assembled with transplanted trees and shrubs. Could we grow together? Would we all thrive? There was so much more to worry about this time—all sorts of stuff, so many people. Back then, the first time, there were only four people at the ceremony (including bride and groom) and the life to be constructed grew out of two very young people, alone.

So this new marriage was externally much more complicated than the first had been. Even the children had endured losses early in life, and the prospect of helping each to move on in a healthy way was daunting. And at the very center was this constant question, "Do you feel married?"

With each passing day, the marriage grows and all of us nurtured by the marriage grow. We are down the road on the journey, I hope nowhere near the end. Sometimes, but not very often, we are alone together these days. We make time for each other in snippets each week and sometimes for a few days in a row, with great scheduling gyrations. There's so much family and professional activity swirling around us that sometimes I hardly know what the heart of the marriage is.

Maybe it's just that quiet little place I can go every week to relax for a few minutes. Later the visits with each other will be longer, as we journey toward a time without children. For now, every night we talk about the progress of these young lives under our roof. We marvel at our joy. The achievements of the children intellectually and physically bring us pleasure every day. We share in their triumphs—making teams, scoring goals, earning respect in the community, and staying academically strong. We have all been very lucky so far.

I would not have thought that this phase of marriage—the raising of a family—could possibly be so much fun.

Why not? Maybe because my mother had to do so much alone, in the isolation of the fifties. I must have been afraid I would be isolated too. Where was my father? He traveled constantly, worked hard, and died young. We five kids barely knew him. I hope this doesn't happen to the father of my kids. I don't think it will. We're watchful and hopeful.

Molly

"I have more to learn from my parents' relationship"

Dear Reader,

In my marriage I fight the ugliness of my parents' relationship. It has become the chip on my shoulder. I passionately strive not to become my mother, the dominated woman. I fight to be heard. I demand equality in every aspect of our life—money, cooking, cleaning, time with friends. I do not stand silent if shouted at. I shout back. I do not tolerate derogatory comments. No one should. It may sound as though I am strong—in many respects I feel I am—but at times this strength turns into unnecessary anger. I am desperately afraid of losing myself in this relationship.

I grew up in a family where shouting replaced discussion and my father was always boss. He worked freelance and always expected my mom to be with him on the days he was not working. My mother has not had a job since she married my father. For many years it was not allowed. When it finally was, she had lost all of her self-esteem and desire for independence. She is a remarkable lady in many respects—intelligent, funny, attractive, exuberant, and patient. But she is insecure about her own self-worth after years of verbal abuse, criticism, and condescension. I, too, suffer from insecurity, much of which I also owe to my dad.

Basically my "chip" is unnecessary. I married a kind, secure, sharing man who supports my independence and encourages my freedom, growth, and individuality. But he, too, is haunted by bad memories of his parents' marriage and is fighting his own demons. Most important, together we have recognized the faults in these marriages

125

and together we are striving to avoid repeating them. We have instituted the "bad-boy/bad-girl jar" in our home, whereby we have each committed to put in a dollar for every impropriety directed at the other—shouting, insults, swearing, anything hurtful. The goal is never to fill the jar.

I am not sure my parents have stayed together because of their love and commitment or because my mother was afraid to leave. I know she has the ability to see the good in my father and the love in his heart. I understand the commitment she made to him and how seriously she takes this. All too often, I think, couples find it easier to divorce than face their problems and work together to solve them. Maybe I have more to learn from my parents' relationship than simply to do things differently.

Mary

"There are certain things we will never say"

Dear Reader,

My parents have been married for over forty years. I cannot judge whether it has been a satisfying marriage, but it has endured through moments of crisis and great pain and so, on some level, it has been a success. In trying to come to terms with my own marriage, I find myself looking back.

From my own observations (and without the benefit of statistically significant sampling or scientific inquiry), it seems that marriages of long duration have rituals that form the fabric of the relationship. As in my parents' case, arguing is an important one.

I often think about the scene repeated year after year in my home during the Jewish holidays. On each holiday my mother and grandmother would spend a frenzied day completing the preparations for the evening meal—cooking and baking, seasoning and tasting, and seasoning yet again. Each holiday morning, as my father left for work, my mother would admonish him to come home early. That evening my father would invariably return an hour late, wilted flowers in hand, muttering about the terrible holiday traffic (which he seemed to regard as a completely unexpected development even though holiday traffic was bad every year).

My mother, of course, would be waiting at the door and, upon my father's arrival, burst into a litany of angry complaints about the ruined meal—how she had worked all day to prepare a wonderful dinner and now the pot roast was overcooked and the vegetables were limp and, worst of all, the family would have to rush through the meal so my father could get to synagogue on time. He would invariably throw up his hands and, in turn, complain about how hard he worked and how my mother always gave him a hard time regardless of what he did. A few minutes later we would sit down to dinner, all the while assuring my mother that the food tasted just fine.

After watching this scene year after year, I finally asked why she just did not prepare a simpler meal or start cooking later in the day, since she knew my father always came home late on the holidays. (And on every other occasion, since my father, as optimistic about travel times as he is about every other aspect of his life, always assumed there would be clear roads and strong tailwinds.) She rebuked me for interfering in an area that was none of my concern and then pointedly informed me that she and my father enjoyed having this argument.

At the time I was puzzled by her response. After all, it did not look like they were enjoying themselves. Now, after more than a decade of being married, I think I understand. The Jewish holiday fight was a safety valve for them, an opportunity to vent their frustrations safely. Since it was, after all, a holiday, they had to make up quickly. Moreover, it had become a ritual for them and gave them a sense of continuity and comfort.

In my own marriage, our arguments have essentially the same theme, which, come to think of it, is not so different from my parents'. Wife to husband: "If you really loved me, you would be more sensitive to my needs (that is, share more of the household burden, give me more emotional support, value what is important to me)." Husband to wife: "If you really loved me, you would appreciate me for who I am, stop expecting me to change, and stop nagging me."

With a high degree of accuracy I can predict we will have this fight (in one variation or another) not on the Jewish holidays but on the first day of any vacation, on Mother's Day (the unnatural reversal of roles creates tension in our house), and before we go out (my husband puts on his oldest clothes, I express outrage, he tells me I am a nag and then changes into something acceptable, something he probably intended to wear all along).

Not only do our arguments have the same theme, but like many other couples, I suspect, our arguments have certain parameters. Fighting is unacceptable in front of certain people—professional associates, in-laws, acquaintances, and even certain friends—and is certainly restrained (but, for better or worse, not avoided) in front of the children.

More important, although we have never acknowledged this to each other, there are certain things we will never say, even in the heat of battle, because we know instinctively that, once said, these words can never be forgiven. The forbidden words relate to those areas the other person is most acutely and painfully sensitive about, the words that, daggerlike, quickly and sharply pierce the heart.

Reflecting on the highly structured, repetitive nature of our arguments, it seems that they actually strengthen our marriage, rather than weaken it. We can let off steam within accepted boundaries, in ways we know will not "rend us asunder." We can secretly mouth the other's expected rejoinders when we begin to argue, and we know when it is time to stop.

In the end, I suppose, what makes a marriage last is not how much you love the other person but how the marriage provides structure, comfort, and predictability in a world that is chaotic, uncontrollable, and profoundly indifferent.

Elizabeth

"The essence of marriage is the ability to share power"

Dear Reader,

The essence of a successful marriage over time is the ability to share power. This requires that power be present on both sides, because if all the power belongs to one person, sharing is not really possible. Sharing power, then, requires planning. Each spouse must do what is necessary to obtain some power and then must be willing to share it.

Even if you are lucky enough to have a lasting, loving feeling, your marriage can fail if your lives are not arranged so each spouse has the maximum chance to respect the other and forgive their inevitable selfish behavior. When both spouses are allowed to make substantial contributions to the relationship, they have concrete reasons to respect, give space to, and forgive each other for their shortcomings.

I am not sure what really goes on in the development of today's relationships between men and women, but thirty or forty years ago relationships were often one-sided and it required some vision of the future to provide for power sharing. The man made a living. The woman made a life. If the man was the center of the relationship in marriage, as was the custom, and the woman's role was to make the home, then her status and power in the relationship were precarious.

If the personalities were such that the husband was dependent upon the wife emotionally, or if she was smarter or more stable than he, then sharing power was more easily accomplished. Each needed the other and as long as nothing happened to disturb the relationship, a successful marriage was possible. However, if there was a glitch, the marriage collapsed because the man really had all the power and the wife's power existed only as long as her husband valued her. She had no real power of her own. If her importance to him changed, the relationship changed. This subtle pressure on the wife tended to make her insecure because she constantly worried whether or not she was necessary.

In my marriage, the traditional way was not a reasonable way to proceed, for several reasons. I am too independent to rely on anyone very much and my wife is too insecure to be in such a tenuous power position and too talented to play a secondary role. Fortunately, we worked out a better arrangement than the one in general use thirty years ago.

I married, in my early twenties, a beautiful and intelligent twenty-year-old. She was the best person I had ever met, and so I married her, even though it was not a good time for us to do so. She was much too young. She had no real plans for her life. I was not really mature. Our relationship was full of love but there was little else to it. I was an intern and she was still in college. Life was not easy, especially for her. I knew the time would come when it would not be enough to be beautiful and in love. She needed to have a life separate from mine so she would value herself separately from us as a couple and I would value her as a person separate from myself. We worked this out together, although we never actually spoke of it in these terms. Later in my life, I encouraged my children to be independent. I wanted them to understand that women—particularly women—need to develop independent strengths apart from their husbands, in order to keep their own and their husbands' respect over time.

When our children were teenagers, my wife went back to school and then studied medicine and became an internist. The process was difficult and required sacrifices on all sides, but over time, it worked. She has been practicing for several years.

There is no doubt that her career has fortified her. She has a much stronger self-image, higher self-esteem, and is more independent. She is happier than she has ever been. I see her as my colleague and equal in ways I did not years ago, and I respect and value her differently. We have more of a partnership, our marriage is stronger and more stable, and in many ways her added power and value make her more important and powerful to me as well. But it is harder to actually live life this way. Things are hard to arrange day by day, details are inconvenient.

The theoretical disadvantages of a two-powerful-person relationship actually become real in the end. It takes some getting used to.

Henry

🦋
"I didn't know if there would be enough love and time"

My dear son,

Your father is so kind, so gentle. As I write this you're snuggled in his arms waiting for *King Kong* or *Godzilla* to come on the video screen. These nights are perfect.

If I go downstairs I might feel hassled. It's a mess. I cleaned several times today and it's still a mess. It's my job to do most of the cleaning up. That's because I'm home—so I can be with you when you need me. It's taken me a few years to get used to doing the household stuff and to realize that your father does a host of things he doesn't want to do at his job.

My parents—your grandparents—encouraged me to get married. They said they just didn't want me to be alone. I didn't know what they meant. I had them, good friends, lots of interests. I was full, and though I hoped I would have somebody to love in my life, I didn't really know, or care, how much better things could be.

My daddy died before your father and I got married. Your father asked for permission to marry me when my daddy was so sick he could barely speak. He nodded yes and my mom was so happy she hugged me. Then my daddy died and your father and I got married. My mom went a little crazy. She seemed very angry with me. I think it was because suddenly everything had changed. Now I was married and she wasn't. She married again and I felt Daddy's presence around me a lot, so everything was fine.

We found out we were going to have a baby. I was happy but scared because I didn't know if there would be enough love and time for all three of us. The love was no problem. The time was. We needed time as a family, as a couple, and each of us (except you) needed to be alone. It took about a year to figure out how to juggle all of this. We still don't always find the time we need.

When you were born, I was happier than I'd ever been. You were everything then that you are now—sweet, alert, inquisitive, funny (and we'd only just met!). One week later my mom was in a coma and we knew she'd die soon. She was old and had lived a pretty good life, but I felt as if I was no longer standing on the ground.

I became terribly worried about your safety. It was hard for me to trust anybody, even your father, to take care of you. I was so shaken it took me a long time to see how good he was with you. The love between your father and me continues to grow. He tries to help me fulfill my dreams. I try to help him with his. He can get me to laugh when I'm crying.

You, my big three-and-a-half-year-old, told me yesterday you want to marry me. Of course, this desire is natural at your age, but I'll let it mean, too, that you know how deeply satisfying being married is. I love you.

Mommy

🐾

"Together we make empty streets interesting"

Dearest Husband,

I sit in the restaurant of our favorite museum in Europe. It is a time of reflection for me and I feel inspired to write. I miss you and I love you.

This is my first trip alone since our marriage, but this trip is different. An old friend is ill and called for help, for me to come and visit. Because you know I love you and am committed to you, you let me go. In between periods of long conversations and intimate discussions, I sightsee. I go to the museums and visit the historic buildings. It is absolutely not the same as doing these things with you.

All of this leads me to think about why it is so wonderful to travel together. We go to have a good time, take a break, learn, and experience. Generally we accomplish all of these ends. Moreover, we always enjoy each other's company and deepen our knowledge of each other. You laugh at me for my elaborate preparations but you enjoy knowing you are cared for. Still, the most important part of traveling together is that we have plain, old-fashioned fun, the warm, constant, having-a-good-time kind of fun. I enjoy having you by my side. I enjoy your presence, your being, kindness, gentleness, humor.

Each of us cares that the other is having a good time, and we share. Together we decide what we most want to see. Then we discover what moves and inspires us. We work in tandem. You drive and I navigate. I plan, you approve and help to execute. And then we have our debriefings. What have you most enjoyed today? What have been the highlights of the trip so far for you? You are delightable and your delight helps mine blossom.

Yes, sometimes things do not go smoothly. Sometimes we upset each other the way we might at home, yet you are committed to settling our disagreements so we can get back to enjoying each other's company. And when external circumstances cause part of a trip to be less than excellent, we do not diminish our own good times.

On Sunday my friend was tired and I spent the late afternoon alone and had dinner by myself. Had I been with you, we would have eaten together. We would have taken a long walk to the restaurant. Alone I was hesitant to do so. The streets were deserted and not inviting for a solitary walk. When we are together we make empty streets interesting. We comment on how the smallest urban details help to illuminate a culture. Alone I note them, but without you to share these observations, my delight and interest in what I see is diminished.

So I miss you now. Traveling together is giving and sharing. I will see you soon. I cannot wait.

Your devoted wife

"We still like to be together and laugh"

Dear Reader,

One of the nicest things about marriage is having someone to play with at home. The first time I met Sam was at his sister's house. He had come from Baltimore, where he worked, to do some buying for his store.

Claire and her husband, Frank, were about my parents' age and were lovely hosts. After some proper chatting and getting acquainted, someone suggested playing charades, and off we went for a fun evening and a lot of laughing. One of the nice things about all of Sam's sisters was that they often giggled—just like me. When the evening was over, Frank suggested a chess game to Sam.

So, on my next date with Sam we played chess, but

I had forgotten how long one game or two could last. After two games, which Sam won, he brought me home past midnight. The next morning I had to explain to my parents that we were playing chess. A year later on New Year's Eve, Sam and I joined friends who also liked games, especially bridge. Horrors! When we looked at the clock it was six in the morning.

My mother told me the next day that it was time to consider marriage. My father said he needed his sleep.

We did get married. We lived in Baltimore and a few years later moved south. Soon we joined a group of bridge players. For several years we used to go away for a long weekend to play in our own bridge tournament. We bought a small silver trophy cup and had our names engraved on it. The winning couple in the tournament would keep the cup for a year and wrap it beautifully and bring it to the next New Year's tournament. We all enjoyed these little vacations together.

Now that some of our friends have died or are too ill to do much, we have not planned a tournament for this year.

However, Sam and I still like to be together and laugh, and we are teaching our grandchildren how to play games and enjoy them. When we visit, we always bring puzzles or some game to play. At the end of the visit we play Monopoly. Sometimes it's Sam and grandson versus granddaughter and me, sometimes Sam and grand-daughter versus grandson and me. We set the alarm clock to ring after an hour. Otherwise we might get home early in the morning again, and we are not quite up to those late hours now.

Carla

"The stresses tore us apart, then cemented us together"

Dear Reader,

Shortly before my husband and I got married, my uncle (who was my legal guardian) turned to my future in-laws and said, "These two are both so stubborn, I don't know how this marriage will survive." My uncle died two years later, but the marriage has survived twenty-four years. I'm not sure how.

When my husband and I were first married, we were both in school full time and worked part time. We were delighted to be husband and wife after two and a half years of dating. We happily shared our household respon-sibilities, including the laundry. My husband did the gro-cery shopping, I cooked, and we both cleaned up. He took charge of the paperwork and financial duties, such as paying the bills and balancing the checkbook. All of our waking hours were devoted to school, work, our small apartment, and each other. We were poor students, but we were content.

I completed my bachelor's degree and received my elementary teaching credential two years after we were married. My husband received his master's degree in economics and decided to continue for his doctorate. The summer he finished writing his dissertation, we decided to have a baby.

I'd taken a one-year maternity leave from my teaching job, so I stayed home with the baby while my husband began looking for steady employment. Since I was home with the baby and had "nothing to do," he began transferring some of his responsibilities to me. First came the grocery shopping, then the laundry, housework, and errands. It was overwhelming at first, especially with a new baby, but I managed, though not always happily.

I threw all of my energy into doing my tasks, which left little time for our relationship. The busier I became, the more outside work my husband took on to fill his time. I never realized that he felt neglected and ignored, replaced by a baby.

When he began traveling on business, he was happier. Then I felt ignored and lonely. I filled my days with play groups, shopping, baby, and household duties. His life seemed glamorous while my work seemed endless. We weren't good at saying what was on our minds, we could have listened more closely to each other, and we didn't recognize each other's signals very well, but we managed to stay together. Maybe out of stubbornness, maybe out of necessity. Those years weren't easy, but they weren't terrible either.

His jobs became more lucrative and our lifestyle acquired the trappings of success—house, sports car, vacations, a cleaning lady. We had a second child, another son to love and care for—a major responsibility.

The more we acquired, the harder my husband worked to maintain what we had. I was often lonely, but I was too busy caring for our family and home to do anything about it. My requests for companionship were viewed either as complaints or as impossible demands.

Through the years we sought counseling off and on for marital problems and child-rearing issues. Counseling taught us to communicate better, and I learned to stand up for myself. We redivided our responsibilities and tried to be more open about our feelings. Life became nicer. Then my husband had a heart attack.

I was afraid. I didn't want him to die, so I decided I had to take better care of him. Suddenly I had all of my old responsibilities plus a new one: taking care of a forty-year-old man who had always been independent but now was being told what he could and couldn't do. "Exercise, eat properly, work reasonable hours, don't get overtired," his doctor and I said. "I won't go out weeknights, I can't attend all the boys' sports activities, I'll only go out one night each weekend," he informed me.

After a year I was tired and angry. I was angry with my husband for almost dying and angry about having to do everything alone. I returned to counseling and, thanks to a wonderful counselor, learned that I didn't have to do everything. What a relief.

I knew I could make decisions on my own. Now I learned the value of sharing decisions with someone I love—my husband. Again, since his heart attack, we're paying more attention to what we need to say to each other and how we listen, and, again, together we're caring for our family and our home. He travels less and spends more time with us. Our sons have grown up to be well-adjusted human beings with good values. I've returned to work full time, not as a teacher but as a journalist, and my husband and I treasure our time together.

Maybe it took us twenty-four years to grow up, grow apart, and then grow close again. Our strength as a couple has been tested during many crises. At times the stresses tore our relationship apart, then cemented us together. The glue that bound our marriage through all these years is our love and respect for each other. Despite all, the marriage has lasted. Maybe our stubbornness helped.

Elyse

"We weathered twenty-eight years of illness"

Dear Reader,

As I look back, I realize how clever I was to have divorced my first husband one month after our daughter was born. I was twenty-one and had been married for all of two years. I didn't know how to articulate or even identify my gut feeling at the time, but I knew with certainty that people don't ever have a basic change of spirit, and an unknown (alone with a baby in a strange city) was better than a known (a depressing, misarranged, lackluster relationship with no potential for future friendship).

As a single woman with a new baby, alone on the West Coast, my family still on the East Coast, no marketable skills, and limited financial resources (could I expect more than a hundred dollars a month in combined alimony and child support when divorcing an attorney seventeen years my senior?), I knew that cynicism was incompatible with the joyous exhilaration brought about by motherhood. So I considered and quickly dismissed the possibility of becoming bitter.

A combination of luck, blessed good fortune, and written-in-the-stars exquisite timing brought John and me together. As we reflected during our fortieth-anniversary celebration this year, we agreed that ours has been a most unique union. Along with our three supportive children, we have weathered twenty-eight years of critical illness with our dignity and humor still intact. As survivors, we never lost understanding and respect for each other's individual coping styles. Well, almost never. The remarkable feature about John's years of well-spaced traumas is that they led to constant positive growth.

Instead of confronting issues head-on, how many did we manage to sidestep, secretly hoping we could rearrange our coping mechanisms to let us deal with our troubles later, after the dust had settled? I guess quite a few.

I remember insisting it couldn't be my husband the hospital emergency room nurse was calling about with some jumbled message because it was Sunday morning and he was water-skiing with the children. My belated, misdirected anger because I'd agreed to buy the boat for the sport I was convinced led to the attack . . . and the pile of guilt that clouded my vision when I wanted to sneak out to the beauty shop while he was still recovering . . . or the panic and fear that if he died I might have to support myself and our three children—me, with no college degree, no marketable skills, and none of his family or mine here in California.

What did we do? We did whatever we had to (within the confines of the doctor's rules) to keep going and stay positive. He mentioned a restriction, we came up with a replacement. Cut out singles tennis—John never played better doubles. He said get plenty of rest—I stuck a mirror under John's chin whenever I thought he'd fallen asleep too peacefully and too quickly. We were given a go-ahead to resume sexual activity—that took a little longer because we were both so hesitant.

We relearned, reexamined priorities, and started to talk—really talk—about everything that troubled us, as we never had before. How terrific and wise he was to unselfishly encourage me to go to college. Four tough years and then a degree. I was able to develop the confidence that comes with knowing I could take care of things, I could make a living writing and editing. The search for a thesis topic began and ended right in the family and materialized into a book. And years later into another book. I found a voice that let me speak out (I think appropriately) whenever I noticed a medical or nursing shortcoming. It was like coming of age.

I wonder how many couples celebrating significant anniversaries reflect and share what they consider the most outstanding features of their marriage. It's enlightening to recall memories that have faded with time but can be summoned for a fresh look from a new perspective.

We're both excited that we celebrated our fortieth year together with a brave new approach to travel. We took our first European trip to see Paris, London—and yes, we played a round of Glen Eagles golf in Scotland.

Living the way we do, life's delicious bonuses, including five sensational grandchildren, are appreciated to the fullest.

Marion

"Who can give us back our joy? Our children"

My love,

Joy—what a wonderful, giddy, noncerebral gift it is to feel really good. What happened to our joy? One or the other of our parents and grandparents mixed up being responsible with being perfect, but there's no point in laying blame. When I was very young my nickname was Sunshine. Clearly something changed. Who can give us

147

back our joy? Our children. They offer us the opportunity to share in their joy and challenge us to help them keep it intact, safe inside for them to draw on the rest of their lives. They don't question the sanity, or sophistication, of someone who asks, "What makes you happy?"

Sometimes during dinner, after we've asked for the umpteenth time that they use forks, drink their milk, keep their hair or cuffs out of the ketchup, I feel we're repeating scenes from our childhoods, joyless, heavy scenes, and I shudder. We missed a lot of fun and laughter while our parents placed importance on everything we did. Then, when I hear the children laughing about something or other and they giggle and hiccup, I'm reassured. Their bright, laughing eyes delight me, but they also warn: let them be themselves, their magnificent, funny, strong selves.

In my heart I know that if we're happier, they'll be happier. If we take time to enjoy ourselves, to giggle and cuddle and put aside responsibilities for a bit, they'll do the same when they're in our shoes. By lightening up we'll make them easier on themselves. Of course, for people like us, weighed down by our expectations of ourselves, held back by long forgotten warnings, just having more fun may be an effort at first. There are good, logical reasons for having fun, but I'd feel silly arguing them. Is this ludicrous?

Life's short, and, having realized the consequences of not changing, I plan on having some good times. I'm even going to learn to laugh at myself.

You're the best listener, so I'm sure you've heard me, and you're a loving man, so I know you care. Am I trying to change you? You bet. I'm leaping out of bounds to save us from ourselves. After you think this through in your customary manner, please leap with me.

Sunshine

"I am thinking of a kind of wanton happiness"

Dear Reader,

During 1992 I made several visits to the Matisse retrospective at the Museum of Modern Art. Each time I walked through with a different companion. And each time we lingered over one of the artist's early canvases, a work called *Conversation*, painted around 1908.

The image shows a man and a woman, evidently in midsentence, in a room of solid blue. (I remember the shade as a saturated cornflower color.) Bitter words have been exchanged, and the moment hangs from a thread—something once alive between them either has just been crushed or is just about to be. The man, standing, wears striped pajamas, his shirt collar tightly fastened. The woman, seated in a small chair, wears a dressing gown, open at her throat. His goatee has been stiffly groomed. Her long dark hair has been slicked back, as if wet from a shower. The man's eyes are fixed on the woman; his lips are nearly shut. The woman's gaze rests on the man; her lips are nearly parted. The usual interpretation of the scene is that it is a marriage on the brink. (Matisse's own marriage was quite troubled around the time this painting was created; the woman resembles his wife.)

Nearly all of my companions fell for *Conversation*, from a friend old enough to be my parent to a child young enough to be my offspring.

One friend who came with me is a biologist, specializing in the physiology of the brain. He and his wife have been married, more or less happily, for seven years. They have one child, a son, who is obviously the light of their lives. My friend's wife is a mathematician. She is also unnervingly empathic, with a kind of X-ray vision for the truth of his feelings. He kids her about that to her face, sometimes brutally, but when she's off on her own he refers to her as indispensable to him, like salt. Today I take them to lunch and offer up one extra ticket to the Matisse show. "Let Will take it," she says. "You fed him, you can have him." She smiles; there is an understanding between them, it seems. He throws her a kiss and comes along.

The crowds at the museum are so thick they seem to suck all the light from the rooms. The paintings look oxygen-starved, unyielding. When we reach *Conversation* we have to wait several minutes for a decent view of it. At last we get a ringside spot.

"This is great!" my friend says, like someone rooting at a game.

"What do you like about it?" I say.

"Everything," he says. "The colors, the composition, the idea."

"What do you think they're saying?" I say.

He sinks into silence, then he says softly, "It's over." I can barely hear him.

"Do you mean that they're saying, 'It's over,'" I ask, "or that their conversation is over?"

"I don't know," he says.

For a while neither of us speaks. I break the ice.

"So," I say brightly, "if you were Matisse, what time of day would you have painted here?"

My friend rises to the bait. He likes "what-if" games.

"Eight," he says, "a.m." Then he adds, "They're at breakfast."

"How do you know?"

"The woman's dressing gown. The French of that period and class wore them only in the morning."

"But the blue is a night color, no?"

151

"No," he says. "It's not. I think it's what people sometimes call a French blue." He peers forward. "I see it's pretty broken up here."

I stare at *Conversation*. Maybe it's really a simple thing after all—a painting about a breakup. Maybe it's only my take on it that makes it seem complicated, opaque.

"Let's walk through the upstairs," I say, "where it's less crowded."

We take off, bypassing room upon room of masterpieces. I scan the walls, searching for the most wonderful thing I can find to point him toward, to lift his spirits. Finally I spot it, a magnificent line drawing of a satyr, reaching for a recumbent nymph. It lifts my spirits too.

"Over here," I sing.

My friend trails me to the drawing, but when he sees it he steps right up and his gaze plunges in.

"Ravishing, no?" I say.

"The satyr's shoulder!" he says.

"The nymph's thigh," I venture.

"And his hands," he says. "So much is in them— lust, fear, tenderness."

"It makes me happy just to look at it," I say.

"You could live with this one forever," he says.

I let my mind wander off leash, wherever it wants to go. It makes a beeline to sex, the first time my husband made love to me. We were very young—kids, really. It was deep summer, the fragrance of honeysuckle every-where. We lay on a narrow bed. Slowly he unbuttoned my blouse. So far, so good. Then he got to the bra.

My mother had taught me to buy sturdy bras with lots of support. Well, sturdy bras have lots of hooks and eyes. They aren't made to be slid off in a narrow bed while you're lying down; they're made to be unlocked like a vault. He got the first hook and eye apart, but the second set wouldn't budge. His face began to flush with exertion. Finally, gritting his teeth, he asked for assistance. I sat up and angled my arms around my back. It wouldn't budge for me, either. So he stood up, and I stood up, and he attacked the problem from a position of leverage. Even that didn't help. At last he gave a yank, then I heard him say, "Uh-oh." The remaining hooks had bounded free, all right, but the eyes were still in them.

My husband and I have been married for a quarter of a century. Both of us have always worked. Once we did exactly the same kind of work, and most of our inner lives went without saying. Paradoxically, that was also when our sex life was the most troubled. About eight years ago our careers diverged, and now we have learned that we must make a conscious effort to spell out and commingle the elements that couple us.

Recently my husband confessed something I'd never known. It concerned a pair of homely brown leather boots that he had purchased during our honeymoon—we went to Maine, where it poured the entire time—and that he still wears.

"Those relics," I said. "Why don't you throw them away?"

"You know why I keep those boots?" he said. "Why I've resoled them, and resewn them, and recovered them with beeswax year in and year out? Because on that trip, apart from some walks through the muddy woods, our life together took place entirely in bed. When I touch the lubricated skins, it's like touching you. When I wear them, it's like wearing our history." The boy who bought those boots could never have conceived such a story; he was much too cocksure. And the girl who married him could never have melted to hear it; she was much too frozen. You can see why physical intimacy between us has grown more frequent and intense. How could it not? It is both the natural conclusion and the epitome of these conversations.

As it turned out, we never got to the Matisse show together. We had planned to visit it, with dinner following, on one of the museum's late nights. At the last minute, however, my husband got tied up at his office. I went to the show without him, but I felt at loose ends and soon left. At home I paid the baby-sitter, undressed, and settled down on the living room couch with a book. My disappointment wasn't a passing matter.

We've been fighting a lot lately. The occasion for the fights is usually money, but I think the real subject is that we can't see each other anymore in the way we once did. This date was the fruit of one of our reconciliations. Tonight my husband doesn't get home until almost twelve. He greets me, undresses, and takes a place on the other end of the couch.

"I missed you very much," I say. "I really wanted to hear your reaction to a couple of paintings." Then I describe *Conversation*. When I finish he says, "I don't have to see it. You saw it for both of us."

I look down at my hands. He stands up, walks over to the rack of CDs, and picks one out. Holding it level, he says, "I want you to be happy. I love you."

But I barely register his words as his. I am thinking about them as *words*: the different tones in which they can be spoken; the different effects according to where the accents fall; the way a vowel, in English, parts the lips, yet a consonant, in French (*Je t'aime*), shuts them. I am thinking of other times he said these words to me and I've echoed them before he finished speaking. I am thinking of the first time I said these words to him, and he looked at me, his face crumpling, and said absolutely nothing. I am thinking of the longing these words can free, and of the meanings they can incorporate, and of works of art where they never appear because they are the essential subject.

I am thinking of a kind of wanton happiness that erupts when you feel whole at your core, so transparently yourself that you let your world look right through you. I am thinking about exactly what color the room in *Conversation* is.

He puts the CD into the machine, presses the start button, switches off the lamp, and sits down. For a time we just listen, unspeaking in darkness, my bare feet grazing his naked thigh. What we hear is Lena Horne—now throatily, now lyrically, now plaintively, now teasingly, now briskly, now with heartbreaking languor—painting the full diapason of the blues.

Felicity

"Marriage does not mean the loss of autonomy"

My darling daughter Catherine,

On Valentine's Day you were feeling a little lonely. I guess the commercialism of the day got to you. You told me something I found interesting: you are afraid of a romantic attachment because it would signal a loss of freedom and autonomy. Did you get this idea from watching your father and me? I certainly hope not.

Marriage does not mean the loss of autonomy. Marriage means becoming part of a unit. With children, the size of this unit grows. It may not be run along democratic lines—indeed, ours is not—but belonging to our family unit means that there are three people who care for you more than anyone else. We expect the same in return.

So, my dear, do not fear romantic attachments. One may be the start of your own family unit. Your marriage will be completely different from mine. You will have more choices. You will also not be able to blame your husband if you make the wrong decisions. I taught you to think for yourself but not to put yourself first. I love you.

Mom

"There are certain requisites for a good, happy marriage"

Donna, my darling granddaughter,

So you have found the man with whom you want to share your life. I am so pleased you sought your old grandfather's counsel. It proves that our relationship is close despite the six thousand miles separating us.

Your fiancé seems like a good person, devoted to mankind in general and you in particular, and I am especially pleased he is an orthodox rabbi. Many thoughts race through my mind as I think about what I can say that might be useful, given our family history. After more than forty years of married life, I do not know all the answers, but I do know this: from generation to generation, conventions change but there are certain basic, fundamental requisites for a good, happy marriage. These include similar cultural, ethnic, educational, and religious backgrounds and at least some common goals and interests.

Marriages are not made in heaven, and for a couple to live happily ever after requires mature contemplation *before* entering into this commitment. Love has its place and is a necessary requisite, but a stable marriage requires more if it is to be a once-in-a-lifetime thing. My parents, your great-grandparents, met for the first time at their wedding, under the chupa. That is the way it was in Europe. Often young couples were married by arrangement through a marriage broker. They learned to know each other and, in time, love each other. Divorce was uncommon, and it was unthinkable in our family. It was a different generation, and marriages in those days were forever, for better or worse. Your great-grandparents' marriage lasted over seventy years. I think they were happy together. Each received certain satisfactions and compensations from the other and this is what a sound marriage ought to provide, is it not?

When your mother and father announced their engagement, they hurt your grandma and me by not heeding our advice. Their differences and incompatibilities were too great for the marriage to endure. In the end, the ones hurt the most were your mother and you. Your father had many good traits but he had no profession or occupation, he had no money, he had no religious upbringing, and he was not observant. We were dumbfounded that our well-educated daughter, who was a highly trained professional, raised in a religious home and taught to appreciate and enjoy our culture, was planning to marry someone from such a different background.

We expressed our reservations and concerns in the strongest possible terms, but she had made up her mind. Within a month they were married, and to avoid pressures and unhappiness they went to the United States, where she worked during the day and took legal training at night in order to pass the bar exam. Like many immigrants, your father became a taxi driver. Despite their efforts, they barely had food on the table. Your father was alone a lot. He became a heavy drinker and he gambled. He went into debt and tried to borrow from family and friends.

Your mother never complained to us. Obviously she was in love with your father and deeply hurt by his actions. After she passed the bar exam, she found a good position with the district attorney's office. Although she was now earning a good salary, he spent it faster than it came in. She continued to try to stabilize him, and just when she thought he was settling down, you arrived. In a last, desperate effort to get him to reform, your mother had a heart-to-heart talk and told him that unless he stopped drinking and gambling, she would leave. His good intentions lasted only a few nights, so she left.

Now, what wise counsel can I offer you? In every good marriage, when problems arise, as they certainly will, there has to be a certain openness and frank discourse to quickly resolve the issues. To remain close-mouthed, keeping matters within, compounds and prolongs problems and contributes to misunderstanding, resentment, and unhappiness. These will haunt the marriage for weeks, months, even years and can undermine and impair any happy relationship. Talking frankly with each other about what is on your mind and in your heart is essential for any stable, lifelong partnership.

There also needs to be a willingness to give and take. Depending on the circumstances and the situation, *both* partners must be willing to give in or give up for the good of the marriage. It takes a very strong person to subordinate his or her wishes and opinions for the sake and love of the other. Over a period of time, if both partners do this, it strengthens the relationship and builds respect.

The truth is, ultimately each couple must find their own way, what works best for them. Now you are about to marry, and you might be interested to know that part of what drew your grandma and me to each other was our mutual desire to break away from our families.

I know you have learned from your mother's experience and have chosen wisely. I am sure you will have a long and happy marriage, with many children, whom you and your husband will love, raise, and educate in the tradition of our fathers and forefathers. I am certain you will make all of us proud and cause us to have good feelings for you and our great-grandchildren to the end of our days. When you marry, you marry more than a spouse. Family relationships matter and add or detract from a happy marriage. This is why we are delighted to welcome your beloved into our family.

Mazel Tov. With God's blessings, I hope to be able to see you this summer under the chupa with your dear David. Until then, with all my love,

Your Opa

"We were dedicated to each other's ideals and truths"

Dear Montana,

I have to admit it's wild for me, wonderful, that you've had this dream to graduate from school and move to San Francisco on your own (where your mom and I landed in the early spring of 1967 with only the dream to *go somewhere*, or maybe not the "somewhere" part, but to go!— dreams seeming a bit more simple then) and that you've actually done it and found a place for your bones and a job, yet—migod, you're cooking. What I love most about it is you knew that to dream at all was half the enactment, the realization, of the dream, and that it was important to dream, to give voice to that human birthright, since any dream helps keep every dream alive. I feel honored, proud to see this so vital in you.

Listening—it's one of the things you've always done best—listening deeply to what you need, or hope for, or hope to give to this world of ours. That's how you find what you have to do. Yes. (To paraphrase Joseph Campbell, following, and endlessly following your bliss. To the essence of what you might be.) It's a bit like what we talked about when I was raising you as a small child and I told you I didn't go to a job like the other dads but had to keep my days open because there were all these poems floating around the universe and if someone didn't write 'em down they were gonna clog the drain. So I needed my days free, see? For that bliss.

And to play with you, my love—that one most of all—one of my dreams and ideals, to raise my child. And so after Mom and I split up because, in part, the direction of our dreams had changed and taken us into vastly disparate areas, and we would live what was true for us, *I got you, babe* (like it said in that old cornball song). I always felt, I always wanted, I always knew it would be one of life's greatest pleasures for me to raise my child. And that's one I was lucky enough to hit right on the head. *Bingo!*

It seems that Mom and I lived, pushed, breathed life into this connection between our own sense of personal integrity and ideals even as it breathed life into us. We were supported by the times, which encouraged the certainty that these things must live if we were to live with meaning, as a people, a species, a world, at all. That the world was the possible, and that we could live out our ideals of what life might be, perhaps not on a grand scale, but certainly in some small way. That to not make the attempt was an act of self-betrayal that echoed the sad lives we saw in the generation before ours.

So into the mouth of possibility we had to go. Stumblingly, to be sure, but hand in hand, Mom and I, each of us leading and following with mutual regard and support—for we really were dedicated to each other's ideals and truths as well as our own. Living this vision was a foundation of our marriage, of the home we made together, and it played out in virtually every aspect of our lives, including the weird, laughable, unpredictable situations and ultimately different directions our lives would take.

I remember when you were two years old and it was Mom's turn to find a job. At the time one of us would work and keep the financial trip together while the other would pursue whatever creative enterprises nourished the soul. She came home from an interview and said that it had gone well, that in fact she had been offered the position but had reservations about taking it.

Picture the conversation: the three of us were living in an apartment with virtually no furniture, sleeping and eating at floor level (our dining room table was a wooden industrial palette that sat squarely in the middle of the living room floor, declaring it an "eating space"), and your mom was telling this to her husband, who wandered around all day writing poetry, thinking about conspiracy theories, and who, it seemed, had more furry hair than the neighbor's overstuffed sofa. I asked her why she didn't want to take the job and she said, "Are you kidding? I'd be working for the Defense Department." (Remember here that I had been doing antidraft work for years.) "So?" I said. "So I'm not sure I could work for them." "Why not?" "Because they're the military, for God's sake, and I don't believe in the military."

"That's not true," I told her. "You're getting us confused. I don't believe in the military. You *do* believe in it. You come from a military family. Your former boyfriend was in the marines. You believe in a strong military defense system for this country." I was using all the persuasive methods I had applied to antiwar arguments over the years and could see she knew what I said was true. "But don't you think it would be hypocritical of me to work for the Defense Department given how we live our lives? How would you feel about it?" "Fine," I said. "It would be hypocritical if I worked for them. But not if you did. We're not the same person. You believe in them. You like them. Take the job."

And, as you know, irony of ironies, I talked her into it. She took the job and has been there fighting for women and minorities within the system for twenty years.

Life.

What's behind this? Only a belief. A belief in freedom, in no politically correct restriction. A belief that each of us must follow our truths as we're able to define them. A belief that we must encourage others to live their truths even if we disagree. For in the end this will keep truth, ideals, and dreams most alive. I know you were raised with this sense of things in our home and in Mom's, and I see it so strongly now in what you bring to your relationship with Bill.

I love you, hon. Remember how it was told that Athena was born out of the brow of her father Zeus? Just another one of the old boy's good ideas? May you add your own page to that myth and continue to be born out of the brow of your own truths and ideals. You honor all things just by being what you are.

Pops

"It was his duty to make sure she earned her degree"

Dear Reader,

My husband and I have two children. He supplied lots of love, joy, and intellectual and cultural stimulation. But when the going got rough, I was left alone to make all of the hard decisions and give all the guidance. I was Major Mom. I was the bad guy. He was perceived, most probably, as passive.

When we had nearly completed raising our children, our younger dropped out of college, declaring she never planned to return to the university, hated the competition, the tests, the drinking environment—and a whole other litany of reasons. My husband has a doctorate and is a college professor. For him, her behavior set off a crisis. He felt it was a crime that with her high IQ, she would not complete her degree. This time, he felt, the problem was too difficult for me, Major Mom, to manage alone. But he did not know what to do.

So, for the first time, he went for help. He went searching for the tools to get his younger child on track. Finally he wanted to help with child rearing and become a better partner to me.

What followed was nothing short of a miracle. He approached our daughter with strength. He approached her situation with fervor. With honesty, forthrightness, and conviction, he told her it was his duty as a father to make sure she earned a college degree—it did not matter what she wanted. He did not care where or how. She had to get this degree and then he would get off her case. Until that point he had never, ever raised his voice or offered direction to either of our children.

The story has a happy ending. She returned to school, earned her degree, and now works. She prefers to forget her unhappy days when she dropped out. Her dad is a fully assertive person now, not only with his children but with everyone. With hard work he has gotten to the core of his emotions. You can imagine how enlivened our relationship has become. He is a truly engaging and engaged person.

Meg

"We needed to talk and reach agreements about our kids"

Dear Reader,

It all seemed so simple. After all, my parents did a great job of raising us. My sister and I are happy and (relatively) well adjusted. We're better educated than our parents and have many more privileges than they ever did. So I, like most of my generation, went to college, had my career, married, and started a family. I married someone who loves me and cares for me, as I do him, and someone who has many of the same values as I. We both love kids and wanted and got our perfect family—a boy and a girl.

At first it worked so well, but then subtly, oh so subtly, our personality and child-rearing differences emerged. When it came to discipline and the children did something wrong, instead of being positive my husband dealt with them in negative ways. My approach was just the opposite: lots of praise and nurturing. So whenever he was negative, I became the buffer and softie (too much of one). Because each of us thought the other was wrong, we became more invested in our own way of doing things. We didn't see the destructive path we were on regarding our children. The children saw that we weren't united and they no longer functioned well at home, although they did fine everyplace else.

Eventually, through family therapy, we learned the importance of listening and respecting each other. We also learned that we needed to talk and reach agreements about our kids, usually compromising, sometimes giving in completely, but always presenting a united front and believing in our final decision. It was hard to buy into this (because we were so sure the other's approach was wrong), but eventually we relaxed and were willing to change.

Now we're both in control. I'm stricter with the kids because I know my husband is much more positive with them. Now I seek his opinions and ideas about the issues we face raising them. He, conversely, listens and trusts what I have to say because I'm firmer. We were able to care enough about each other and our children to make a positive change, one that I hope will affect all of us, as individuals and as a family, forever.

Robin

"Our child has become the reason for our marriage"

Dear Reader,

Marriage—what is the meaning? Well, I know there are many interpretations, including my own. I never had a role model that quite fit the bill for an ideal marriage. I saw two people who didn't like each other and stayed together only for their children. Needless to say, they did more damage to us by staying together than they would have by divorcing.

I married at twenty-five and never felt a hundred percent sure of my decision. I can't really distinguish the reasons why. Was it my fear that we'd eventually dislike each other, same as my parents, or did I just not have it in me?

Our first year of marriage was a rocky road. I now had to answer to someone as well as think of someone else before I made a decision. I also started a business on top of my full-time job, a little added stress on top of the normal marriage agenda. The new business ended after the first year, but it ended successfully and was for the best.

After the first year we had the hard times that some couples go through. I mean the ill fate of cancer to one of our parents. The watching, deteriorating, waiting for the dreaded moment, which took two years. We gave a lot of our time to his parents and became very serious at an early age.

We nurtured what we did have in common and looked forward to building a family together. After two years of marriage and feeling prepared financially and professionally to embark on a family, we had a daughter. What we planned and expected didn't happen. We were given a child with very special needs. She fought for seven months to stay alive and consequently her parents learned the same thing: fight to stay alive.

No one is ever prepared for such a life change. Our precious daughter brings new meaning to life, let alone the word marriage. We now live for the moment and have ceased looking into the future, which can bring anxiety and problems on top of it all.

Our daily routine includes two full-time jobs, transporting our child to and from her rehab hospital, cooking dinner, preparing her nightly ritual before her nurse comes in, and taking care of our enormous paperwork overload from her medical coverage. Our day is never done.

Marriage, very ironically, has become a way to help our child stay healthy and give her every opportunity that's available. In essence she has become the reason for our marriage.

Mary

"The sign for stepmother is 'fake mother'"

Dear Reader,

Stepmotherhood. I always thought I'd have a child of my own to raise from infancy onward. This has continued to be an ongoing painful issue as I find myself in middle age, trying to understand why I'm without my own birth children. But I certainly did find a way to have children in my life.

Stepmotherhood. I wouldn't trade my husband for anyone else in the world. He came into my life with an ex-wife and two children. It's my good fortune that I've known my stepchildren since they were three and one. And though I was out of their lives for a few years, our relationship was renewed when they were at such adorable ages, six and four.

Stepmotherhood. In sign language, the sign for stepmother is "fake mother." But in my heart I hope my stepchildren will know, one day, that I'm not fake. I'm an honest, involved, loving, caring, affectionate person in their lives. I love them very much and I'll have the pleasure this year of giving a birthday party for my stepson, who calls me Benita and has grown from giving me weak hugs, which we shared laughter about as a family, to hugging with all of his twelve-year-old strength and giving me kisses, way near my ear, and talking about how much he likes spending time with me because we talk and I'm "interesting."

Stepmotherhood. Wow, not always an easy journey or an easy place to be. But would I trade it? No!

Benita

"My tongue has bite marks on it"

Dear Reader,

I happen to be quite independent and don't mind giving my husband the reins, but this man I adore thinks he's a technician, electrician, plumber, carpenter, and so on. In fact, he's none of these. My tongue has bite marks on it from all the times I've held in comments when I'm watching TV and he feels compelled to fix the picture. Why can't he do this when he's watching? This is exactly what my father did to us as kids. It got to the point where we preferred to look at fuzz on the screen than tell Dad.

We're renovating our house and my husband purchased an electronics system that he insisted would be fabulous. Of course, he had to install it himself. Well, we've been here five months and this fabulous system still doesn't work. The TVs come on whenever they want to and the answering machine is allergic to the new phone and refuses to record messages. He feels insulted when I point these things out, so he spends hours in our small electrical closet, swearing, wires all over the place, determined to take care of this himself. I'm stuck. I've even thought of hiring someone on the sly to fix this mess.

Halfway through the renovation, we had to make decisions on carpeting for the bedroom. I found a carpet I loved in a color that perfectly matches our wallpaper, but he thought it was too expensive per square foot, although the total additional cost would've been insignificant. We were on a budget, so I don't understand why he made such a big deal, but he thinks the carpet business is a scam. I searched for new carpet and found nothing of interest but the carpet I loved. He, who can't tell the difference between green and blue, accompanied me to the carpet store and picked out a carpet, which I agreed to because I wanted to end this ugly chapter in our renovation experience.

I bit my tongue when it arrived. When the carpet was laid, I hated it. He must realize that it doesn't match the wallpaper, but he says nothing, and I haven't said anything because I don't want to reopen this chapter.

Sally

"I gave him my decision: smoking for gambling"

Dear Reader,

I'm writing about a decision that proved to be one of the best my husband, Mike, and I ever made. To go back to the beginning . . .

My family was transplanted in the early 1920s from northeastern Arkansas to Miami for my father's health. My mother had to support the family. Fortunately she had a teaching degree. The summers found us in Tallahassee because she had to attend a college there to get an additional degree and we lived with a family on their farm. We three city children had wonderful times riding the farm horses, swimming in a nearby lake, climbing trees, prowling the woods. I learned to smoke grapevine and corn silk and enjoyed every puff. Back in Miami, I continued the pleasure, for by this time I had a small allowance.

When I went to college I smoked, as did everybody I knew. Why not? It was considered chic, glamorous, mysterious to have smoke curling around one's face.

Mike and I were married in 1948. He'd never smoked and didn't like to see me do so. I managed not to in his presence but continued to smoke at every opportunity. He, of course, nagged me constantly to stop.

I vividly recall the setting. It was a fall Sunday afternoon. We were sitting on the back porch and he was once again berating me about my smoking. Finally I said, "Okay! Okay! I've decided. Someday I'll think of something I want you to give up and we'll both give up these pleasures at the same time." He agreed. Both of us would change.

Pondering what I could ask him to forgo didn't take long, for I knew the joy of his life was gambling. For years he'd been addicted to the horses, dogs, jai alai, poker, blackjack, or whatever came along. I gave him my decision: smoking for gambling. He agreed. On Decision Day, I gave him my cigarettes and I've never smoked since. Years later, I relented about his gambling when we'd be in Las Vegas, Atlantic City, or aboard ship. Surprise! He soon said gambling wasn't fun anymore because he knew I was breathing down his neck.

How do I feel about all this? No doubt we've saved a lot of money and perhaps our marriage. Our children and their families don't smoke or gamble. Mike and I are now in our early old age, and he probably saved my life. It's heartbreaking to lose friends of many years to lung cancer and emphysema. We agree that this is one squabble that's had a happy ending.

Kathy

"Money became a wedge between us"

Darling,

It's funny how the money problem came up, went away, and then came back again.

When I asked your father for permission to marry you, I was very up front (and nervous) when I said, at the beginning of our marriage, that I wouldn't be able to support you in the manner to which you were accustomed. I didn't know how he would respond, nor do I remember now what he said, so it couldn't have been very negative. When he bought us our apartment, I wrestled with this, but privately I said I would repay him.

My business was doing great and I'll never forget the thrill I felt going on an Easter vacation that cost as much as I made my first year of work. I was so proud I could afford it.

After a while, business wasn't so good, and for the first time in my life I started to have doubts about my ability to succeed. At the same time, all of our friends were doing phenomenally, which accelerated the decline of my self-esteem.

I couldn't deal with talking to you about it because it would have been like saying I was a failure. My brother reminded me that not doing well financially was covered in the marriage vows by "in sickness and in health"—you had vowed to love me no matter what and I had to talk to you because I was in pain. When I finally told you how upset I was that I didn't feel I could talk to you, you responded sensitively, but you were guarded. I'll never forget this. It was then that I realized that money was also a problem for you, and the lower I felt, the more money became a wedge between us.

As we both know, our sex life deteriorated, and if we hadn't discussed it and agreed to seek help together, I don't know what would have happened. Therapy helped us open up many of the doors we had closed. Money may continue to be an issue, but, happily, it's no longer a problem and our sex life is improving. I've come to realize that money was our metaphor for failure.

I still grapple with the concept that your money is our money, but as my self-esteem grows and our income reappears, I feel less and less guilty about spending. I hope we can demonstrate to our children that the money they have and the money they'll inherit is a privilege, not a birthright. That it's okay to enjoy it, not be a slave to it, and use it to better conditions for mankind. When I read this sentence, I sound pompous and self-righteous, but I mean it with all my heart.

Jim

"I have him back again"

Dear Reader,

I was having lunch with three bright, upwardly striving young women when one of them asked why I'd moved to California. I'd been holding court with stories of my years climbing the ladder at a big New York advertising agency and they were impressed. And, frankly, I was enjoying it. "Well," I explained, not thinking twice about it, "Jerry, my late husband, was having some health problems. He was sixty-two and felt he'd worked long enough and we had the house out here, so we moved."

I could feel the shock going around the table. Donna, the most successful of the three, with a flourishing literary agency to her credit, put it into words: "You mean you gave up a job like that because your husband wanted to move?" I could feel every feminist nerve in her body quivering.

"It was part of the contract," I said. "He was there for me when I needed him, so how could I not be there for him?" I guess, instinctively, I'd put it into business terms. But, of course, I wasn't talking about a business contract. It was a moral one, a philosophical one.

"When we were first married," I said, "and my son

had a breakdown, we spent the equivalent of Jerry's whole salary that year to pay for the best medical and psychological help we could get. Jerry was a giant. He said he'd beg, borrow, or steal to pay for it. He said, 'I wanted a family, and when you have a family you have problems.' Well, we were still a family eighteen years later. It was just the problems that were different."

It had been a second marriage for both of us. I'd been divorced for twelve years when I met him, he'd been divorced for three months. It was a blind date arranged by someone neither of us particularly liked. But it worked—I was already using the editorial "we." We started talking the first night he called and didn't stop for eighteen of our twenty-five years together. A couple who met us on our first date later told us they knew we'd get married.

I made far more money than he did, but that never mattered. It was never a question of his or mine. I remember one day standing in the lobby of my office building with a few of the younger women in the group I supervised. For some reason I mentioned that I didn't even sign my paycheck, I just gave it to my husband and he signed it. They were shocked. I explained that I had American Express, Visa, and every department store charge card I wanted. He gave me an allowance whenever I needed it, I had my own checking account, I never had to justify a purchase, never had to pay a bill. I had someone to manage the money. I didn't mind. Nor did I mind that I made most of the money. We each did what we did best.

Jerry was the smartest, funniest, most interesting man I'd ever met. On vacation we'd spend every hour together for four or five weeks and never get tired of each other. But ultimately it was like the joke: "My wife and I had eighteen wonderful years together. Unfortunately, we were married for twenty-six." His health deteriorated when we moved to California. He had a multiple heart bypass and his diabetes became severe. Sadly, the physical ailments were the smallest part of it. He couldn't handle the combination of retirement and illness and went to pieces psychologically.

I had no family out here and all of our old friends were back East, so I had nobody with whom to share our problems. There were times when it was so rough I slid into a depression of my own. And I thought about leaving him. I still wasn't too old to start a new life and he was so difficult, none of our new friends would have blamed me. Don't ever think, when you marry, you're going to change someone. Marriage and time only seem to intensify the things you don't like. Why can't the good things intensify?

When he died, I must admit that my first feeling was relief. He'd become so paranoid and obsessively afraid of death that we were constantly in and out of the emergency room. I went to a luncheon a few days later, and when a friend asked how Jerry was, I said very calmly, "He's dead."

It took a long time to get over my anger at what he'd done to our last eight years. I know now that I should have made more of a life apart from him, but that was my problem, not his. It was only when I started to clean out the closets that I remembered why I'd fallen in love with him. So now I have him back again. And I'm glad I was able to give him a few years in this beautiful place to end his life.

Vivian

"If you never received love, how can you give it?"

Dear Reader,

In ten days my parents will be celebrating their forty-second anniversary. Will my son Dan, who sleeps peacefully in his crib in the next room, be able to announce with pride in the year 2020 that his parents are about to celebrate their forty-second anniversary?

Tears are rolling down my face, wetting the keyboard, when I think of the answer. I hope they create a

182

power shortage in the computer so I won't have to keep thinking. Neither a blackout nor an earthquake would be able to ease the pain and frustration I feel. They might postpone the ongoing crisis but I would still wake up the next morning to familiar scenery.

If I could paint a marriage, what color would I use? What images would I create? Probably I would scout some museums and borrow the images of history—di Cosimo, *The Discovery of Honey*. Munch, *The Scream*. Cezanne, *House in Provence*. Hogarth, *The Graham Children*. The dream picture I see for my marriage is Picasso's *Peace*.

Whoops, I must stop! The baby has just awakened, crying.

I'm back after comforting and hugging him. I restored his need for security and he dove back into the world of dreams. Marriage doesn't bring this original unconditional love most of us get from our parents. Who cuddles me when I have a bubble in my tummy?

Being married to a doctor makes it even worse— you're the last patient on the list. Joe was conditioned to become a physician, to fulfill family expectations. He had to save the people his parents lost. My "outlaws" were so busy trying to reach their goals, they forgot there was a child in need of love, fun, games. If you never received love, how can you give it?

I don't trust Joe to be alone with Dan. He's irresponsible. He doesn't read about or understand child development. He thinks after he permits, and he erased the word "no" from his vocabulary. A child needs boundaries; he teaches none. Also, when he's paged, the call becomes his focal point. He becomes deaf and mute to his immediate surroundings, including the baby.

Otherwise he's a sweet, loving father who bonded nicely with his son. Dan adores his father, but I don't think he misses him even though they see each other very little. I made it a ritual for them to spend time together in the morning. No matter what time Dan wakes up, I change him in our bed and go down to warm up his formula. Then Joe gets up to feed and be with him until he leaves for work.

On many levels my husband wants to learn, but the fear of the unknown is bigger than the ease of learning. When our son was born and through the first six months of his life, my husband couldn't tell him he loved him. "He knows I love him," he kept answering me. As the baby progressed in his milestones, so did my husband. By the time our son had crawled, the words "Daddy loves Dan" echoed through the house.

Guess what, my dear husband just called, announcing over the cellular phone that he'll be home way past midnight. He wanted to know if our one-year-old pulled any new tricks today. I gladly volunteered one. "He walked by your picture and stuck his tongue out." Do I sound hurt, angry, humorous, or simply stupid? Yes, all of the above.

I must say, Joe's a good and generous man. He's hardworking and has a great deal of responsibility. But marriage is also a job with responsibility. A marriage is never a fifty-fifty deal. There are times when one spouse gives forty and the other sixty. There are other times when it's eighty-twenty. Like nature, we all go through cycles and seasonal changes. The leaf must fall off for the tree to rejuvenate and the soil to be fertilized.

We, earth's most civilized and advanced creation, marry, and I don't understand why. Are we the most civilized? Many years ago I came across Nahaman Bialik's vivid ballad "The Wolf," about the Holocaust. Even the wolf was horrified, astonished, and ashamed of the most systematic slaughter and vicious man-made atrocity. Am I comparing marriage to a holocaust?

Should divorced individuals be called marriage survivors or should married people be called married survivors?

By looking back at my previous paragraphs, I think my unconscious unraveled the cause of my disharmonious relationship. My dear husband is the eldest son of Holocaust survivors. They taught him to use various distancing devices, false analogies. He believes in the most primitive psychological form of defense, which is denial. He's passive and waits in the hope that he won't have to come to terms with reality.

I'm a second-generation Israeli who was raised as free as a bird with no fear of concentration camps or annihilation. I believe in prevention. I'm an air force brat and learned to gather intelligence, analyze findings, recognize facts, make assessments, and interpret their implications. I gained mastery by safeguarding against real danger.

How can our marriage survive the continuous battle of his destructive drive and my life drive?

Most essential of all, with a great deal of love and planning, our marriage produced a healthy seven-pound-five-ounce baby, whom I dearly love.

Greta

❦

"A happy marriage requires a lot of hard work"

Dear Reader,

I met my husband at a friend's birthday party when I was nineteen years old, and though we liked each other very much, this was not love at first sight. Later he used to tell me he knew immediately he would marry me one day, but actually we gave ourselves plenty of time. We were engaged two years after we met and married three months later. We got to know each other and found we shared a lot of ideas and interests, especially a love for music. I often played the piano for him, and we went to many concerts and operas together. We also liked to take walks and hikes in the woods around Vienna, alone or with friends. I loved picking wildflowers, he loved great old trees, and soon each of us shared the other's passion. This happened many times in the course of the years, and we always felt richer for it. We talked about our lives and experiences before we met and became, and always remained, very good friends with each other's families.

A marriage can be strained or strengthened by bad times. When Hitler invaded Austria, we tried to emigrate to America with our teenage daughter. Although there were occasions when it would have been easier had we separated, we were determined to stay together. We left everything behind and barely reached England, where we found temporary refuge before the war broke out.

During this time my husband and I learned to trust each other's judgment by discussing our practical and personal problems and by making decisions together. In this way both of us shared responsibility and could support, rather than blame, each other, whatever the result. At the end of these years of constant danger and considerable hardship, we found that surviving our sorrows, cares, and frustrations had brought our family even closer together.

After the war, we finally came to New York City to build a new life. Many old friends were already here. They told us women could find jobs quickly, even if they had never worked, because they were willing do anything, whereas it took the men a long time to find work in their own fields or train for new ones. This created a lot of problems, as husbands began to feel inferior to their wives or as if they had to compete with them. Besides, the idea of a woman working instead of being at home was a major adjustment for many European families. We saw strong marriages falter under the impact of these pressures.

I went to work for the first time in my life. My husband got a job shortly after I did by accepting the first thing that came along, but we knew he would soon want to do something more in line with his abilities and experience. When he decided to make the change, all of our friends thought he was crazy to give up a secure, if inferior, position. However, we had, as always, discussed the situation thoroughly and come to the conclusion that with one of us still working, the other should not settle for a frustrating, unsatisfactory occupation. We both moved into better jobs many times throughout the years. We did not feel the need to prove anything to anybody, so we could take chances and feel secure in the knowledge that we had each other's support.

At the time I grew up, girls who did not find husbands were regarded as failures. Many of them married just because it was expected. I always felt lucky to have found a man who became not only my husband but my best friend and inseparable companion, someone with whom I shared my thoughts and feelings, knowing he would understand and respect them. We were married for fifty-two years, and we were happy.

It is said that happy marriages are made in heaven. I think this means we need so much good luck to find one right person among all the millions of people in the world that heaven has to be our guide. At such times my daughter likes to say, "Yes, but it takes two to make a marriage."

Helen

"There is a contentment now"

Dear Reader,

I am sixty-two years old. I am a survivor. I survived the Holocaust and survived some marital wars. There is life after surviving.

We were kids, he was the boy next door. Then came the war. He returned from Bergen Belsen, I returned from Budapest. I was fourteen going on thirty-five. He was twenty, recovering from typhoid, still hoping that maybe, somehow, a member of his family had survived.

I was seventeen when, in spite of too many obstacles, we did get married and went to South America. I am sad to say it did not work. We were desperately unhappy. He became abusive, started drinking, womanizing, beating me, and so on. I found solace in other men. We desperately loved our two babies.

At twenty-four I was alone. I had lost everything, including my babies.

At twenty-six I met a quiet, gentle man. He was handsome, Jewish, rich, eighteen years my senior, a bachelor. We married. He wanted nothing but a quiet, unassuming existence. I was young and restless and wanted to live. We had children, we moved to Canada. We fought constantly. He suffered—did not like his job and worried, worried, worried. I tried to please him, to bring him out of his shell, to make him happy, feel secure, loved. He could express his love for me only sexually. We did not communicate, did not share. He was stingy with words of praise, affection, money. I begged for counseling. I wanted the marriage to work. I kept telling him we were the most fortunate people on earth—health, energy, beautiful children, position, looks, brains, financial security. All of this finally in a marvelous country, everything going for us.

One day I'd had enough. In my mid-forties, all the children practically grown, I said, "This is it. I can't take it anymore. Get out." He did. Very surprised, but he did. A gentleman. When the lawyer asked me, "What happened?" I told him, "I could not take any more of this five thousand years of Jewish suffering. I want to laugh, live, be happy." My husband reproached me, "All these years I did nothing but worry about you and the children." I replied, "You should've worried less and enjoyed us more. It wouldn't have come to this." He was stunned. I acquired a boyfriend and things went quite well for a few years.

Then our oldest daughter announced her wedding plans. My ex-husband and I had not seen each other since our court hearing for the divorce a couple of years prior. At the wedding he looked at me with so much longing and so much love, my heart broke. I was surrounded by all my children and my mother, but I could see and feel nothing else but his passionate longing. We made love after the wedding and then talked until the sun came out. Yes, we wanted to get back together. Yes, we still had a lot of feelings for each other. Yes, he would go for counseling.

He did. The rabbi was kind, reassuring; we were full of hope. We had a simple wedding under the chupa in the rabbi's study, something we never had before. It was magic.

Eleven years have gone by. We've been blessed with five grandsons. We share, talk, and enjoy each other's company. We travel, go to the theater, attend concerts, study, read books, and are sometimes simply astonished by the mysterious ways God works. I had an interrupted childhood. I was never young. I grew up and was matured by blow after blow, but there is a contentment now, with the fires banked, the sands of time blunting the pains and passions of youth, and yes, I am a survivor.

He will turn eighty this year. May God grant us a few extra years to replace those we foolishly frittered away and denied each other.

Vera

"There is an abyss dividing us"

Dearest,

It seems impossible to me that this month we will cele-brate our twenty-fifth anniversary. I don't feel nearly old enough—and I hope I don't look it, either! I look back with pride and happiness at the years we have spent together, at the lives we have built together, and most of all at our beautiful daughter. I know in my heart you are my soul mate. I have never doubted my love for you or the choice I made in marrying you.

At the beginning, ours was a typical young love—full of dreams and passion. Well, some of the passion may have faded, but the dreams have mostly become a reality. You have earned my unqualified admiration as a lover, provider, and father. Best of all, you are an honorable person. I cannot think of a higher compliment.

There is something that troubles me deeply, as I know it troubles you. Since our son died, I have watched you become consumed with anger. The anger is so pervasive that it spills over into everything—our relationship, your relationship with our daughter, everything. I feel there is an abyss dividing us, drawing you down. I worry that you will never get over this, that you will destroy yourself and our family in the process.

For my anniversary present, I want only this: I want you to devote the time and energy it will take to work through your anger. I mean this with all my heart. You cannot continue to hide behind your work. You must not continue to push people away. Yours is a sensitive soul full of grief and desperately in need of healing. I thought time would be enough, but it is not. Please do this for me, for yourself, and for our daughter.

Anne

❦

"You lift my spirits every time I see you"

Dear one,

Airplanes, where time is capsulized, and anniversaries, when time is celebrated, come together on this flight from Phoenix. While I've enjoyed the last few days in Arizona—the meetings, the golf, the people—a part of me was missing and that part is you. I can't speak for how other men feel when they're away from their wives, families, and homes, but for me the expression "Home is where the heart is" says it all.

And when I think of home, I think of you. You are home for me. You are heart. You make it all worthwhile. Your happy, upbeat spirit is a joy. You lift my spirits every time I see you.

Can you imagine we've been married nineteen years next Sunday? Can you believe how we've built our lives together? When I met you I was spiritless. I was confused about a lot of things, and I was sad. Having recently been divorced, I didn't trust anyone and I was unwilling to make myself vulnerable to the possibility of being hurt again.

I wasn't sure I wanted another commitment because I didn't know if I could tie myself down again.

But there was a quality about you that enchanted me, and despite all the things that have happened to us in nineteen years, happy and sad, that enchantment continues, stronger and more exciting than ever.

This past year has been particularly trying for you with the loss of your mother. Somehow you rise above it and your spirit continues intact. You are wonderful.

If one were to believe in divine gifts, which I do, then God gave you to me. You are the most perfect gift. You are everything I need. You feed my soul and you make my life more happy than it has ever been before.

I have only two complaints. We don't see each other as much as we need to, and we don't find enough opportunities to take advantage of the things we both enjoy. We have become too busy, and probably I'm most responsible for this. Let's work together to change our priorities, because our best and happiest moments are when we share time and experiences together.

Do you remember when we were dating and I used to write to you? I often signed the letters at the end, "From my heart to your heart." Well, my heart has changed since then. You have transferred some of your spirit to me and it's now a happier, kinder, more open heart. I like it better this way. It feels better and fits better. Thank you, darling, for your help in its development.

Happy nineteenth anniversary. Thank goodness we'll be together to celebrate. May it be this way always. From my heart to your heart.

Jack

"We won't have the time, so we must make the time"

Dear Jane,

This weekend Bill and I celebrated our twentieth anniversary, and it was probably the most important one of all. I've always loved our anniversaries. It's become a date to remember the major events of the year (wonderful and sad), close doors on mistakes, and put our relationship in perspective.

It's so easy to get preoccupied with our needs and wants during daily living. I get annoyed by his irritating little habits, he feels hurt when I promise to do something and forget, and we both get resentful about hard things like compromising ("giving in," when I have to do it; "being reasonable," when I want it to come from him). Every year we talk, and it always comes back to the same issue. We feel stressed and misunderstood when we don't have enough time. Time together, time by ourselves, just time. This year we decided to do something about it. For our anniversary we stayed home. Friday night and all day Saturday and Sunday.

We didn't answer the phone (this is hard). We didn't turn on the TV (easier than expected). We didn't look at the mail (what a relief!). We didn't do any chores, yard work, or fixing. We went to the grocery store Thursday night and stocked up on lots of salad stuff and frozen things and fun food for easy eating. So during the weekend we didn't do any of the ordinary daily living things that are always there to distract us and that fill up so much time. Friday night was great. We felt reprieved from all of our responsibilities, with a touch of giddiness and a hint of guilt, like we were getting away with something. We agreed not to talk about work, the house, relatives, or money. We had a long, leisurely picnic dinner on the floor of the living room, listening to music. Listening—the music wasn't just background noise for our talking. Amazing.

It wasn't easy. We kept catching ourselves, or each other, bringing up some bit of chronically unfinished business (next week we have to call the insurance company, plumber, etc.) or recycled personal news (I talked to Bob, Sarah, Ted, your mother today and she or he said . . .). It became clear that our conversations had taken on a pattern of reacting to other people and outside events.

Weren't we once more innovative—and interesting? That's when we got into our discussion about time.

Our time is filled with careers, home keeping, social obligations (both the required and fun kinds), television, computers, and a continuous barrage of temptations from movies, malls, and new and improved things to try.

We've forgotten—or never learned—how to just be. We never have the time to linger in a garden, park, or art gallery. We have many old friends who live within a day's drive whom we never see—none of us has the time, but we keep promising one another that "some weekend this fall . . ." We live by the clock, everywhere. Our creativity has gone into our work (which we both love), but it's all outside of us. We have no balance. Even our relaxation and fun are scheduled and pressured by time.

We spent most of Saturday sitting in our backyard, which is lovely. We usually just look at it in passing or glance at it over the newspaper. We ate brunch there, and lunch, and even napped for a while. We could hear the messages piling up on our machine, and this kept us a little on edge. So we cheated a little—we listened to messages twice a day.

We talked about our personal yearnings. I can't even draw a tree, but I've always wanted to paint. And I've wanted to make quilts but don't have the slightest idea how to begin, and I haven't had time to find out. Bill has spent years waiting for time to take guitar lessons and rekindle his love for photography. Each of us had assumed that somehow time would automatically open up, or that maybe when we retired . . . We attacked our assumptions with great vigor. Who was going to step in and give us this time we craved? How would we feel if we got to retirement and didn't have the health or opportunity to ever dabble in some creative adventures? What about the next twenty-plus years before retirement?

Saturday evening we left the house and drove to a secluded lookout to watch the sunset. We lingered there, holding hands on a park bench. It was magical.

By Sunday we realized we have to do something about our lives. We love each other deeply, we're best friends, and in a crisis we're always there for each other. But somehow we've lost our vitality, our spontaneity, our personal creativity. Our lives aren't in balance, either for ourselves or for each other. When we're stressed with our own frustrations, we often take it out on each other. We don't want to live this way anymore.

Our goal is to really examine our work lives, and within six months we'll take Fridays off to be together, whether it's going and doing or just hanging out. We need to know we'll have sustained, unhurried time with each other on a regular, predictable basis. We know we won't have the time, so we must make the time. It'll never happen without major surgery to our busy lives.

We've been living but we haven't been growing, so we're each going to do some personal expanding. This is exciting stuff. And so my first project will be to make a quilt for you, because you're my best friend and you'll be celebrating your tenth anniversary in a year (which is about how long this will take—if it's small) and because you'll love it even if it isn't perfect.

This was the best weekend of my life.

Pru

"I wish we had more time to just be together"

Dear Reader,

When Mark comes home, the cat doesn't know him.

After six months of marriage, we already have a routine. Mark comes through the kitchen door, drapes his garment bag and briefcase on the counter, holds open his coat. I slip my arms around his waist. We hold each other and say, "I missed you." The cat sits on the linoleum and looks up at us. Finally Mark releases me and squats down. "Hey, Casper. Hello, little one." He pats the cat once, picks him up, and cradles him in his arms. Casper lies still, but he looks at me.

When the cat starts to squirm, Mark strokes his soft, white belly. I say, "I let him down when he does that."

Mark strokes Casper's belly some more. He says, "He doesn't like me."

"He's just not used to you." I smooth the cat's forehead with two fingers. For a moment he relaxes.

Usually it is late when Mark gets home. We are both tired. I ask him how business went and when he has to go back to the client. It is always too soon. We go to bed and he turns to me. He curls around my side, then he nudges me, inch by inch, toward the edge. "You're taking up too much room," I say. I am used to stretching my arms and legs in the big bed, lying diagonally, switching sides.

"There's always more room by you," he says. "Maybe he'd sleep next to me if he had enough space."

I look for Casper. He is lying in the hallway, just outside the door. When we turn out the light, he slinks across the carpet, circles the bed, and jumps on my pillow. He settles himself on the corner and curls into a ball. His tail brushes my cheek.

Casper is in love with me. It is really not fair. After all, Mark was the one who found him, the one who talked me into taking him. But on those rare times when Mark and I are both in the house, I am the one Casper trails.

Mark tends to his "projects" whenever he is not traveling. He gets home from work late. We rarely eat dinner before eight-thirty. Then he disappears into the basement, where he builds, fixes, or installs things. He is a born homeowner, living on a hotel dweller's schedule. I wish we had more time to just be together. He wishes he had more time to do all the things he has to do.

Mark finds me sitting on the living room couch, reading old newspapers. Casper, lying next to me, lifts his head for a moment before stretching into a new position along my leg. "Want to see what I've done so far?" Mark asks.

I save my place with my finger and look up. "As soon as I finish this article." Mark scowls at me and walks away.

"I'm in the middle of a paragraph," I call after him. "You can't expect me to drop everything whenever you feel like it."

I read slowly, then put down the newspaper and head for the basement. Casper runs at my feet. Downstairs, he sniffs Mark's half-built shelves. Mark smiles at me, puts down his tools, and strokes the cat. Casper ignores him, swats at nails instead. "He only comes when you're here," Mark says.

Sometimes I stay with Mark while he works. I talk to him, read aloud, or just sit there. Sometimes he takes a break to watch TV. I tape a couple of programs for him every week. I sit through them again, just to feel his feet on my lap, to stroke his hands, to hear his laugh. If I try to leave, he presses his feet down harder. "But I have things to do," I say. He pushes himself toward me. He bends his legs over mine, holds my waist in his hands, puts his head on my shoulder. I stay.

Casper wakes me at six o'clock every morning. He taps my cheek with his paw, adding the slightest prick of a claw if I do not open my eyes. I grumble and push him away.

The day Mark is leaving, Casper abandons me after a couple of pats. He climbs over the blanketed mound of our bodies and settles himself along Mark's stomach. Mark props himself up on an elbow and runs his hand along the cat's soft side. "Hey, little one." Casper purrs loudly. Mark looks at the clock. "But I have to get up now. I have to pack. I was here all night—why did you wait till now to come over?"

The cat closes his eyes and keeps purring. I roll over and curl myself along Mark's back. I slip my hand under his elbow until I feel Casper's fur. For that one moment, we are all together.

Grace

"We don't have sex often"

Hi there,

How come everywhere I look—magazines, talk shows, books—married couples are said to be having sex, on average, three times a week?

Who *are* these couples? How *long* have they been married? How *old* are they?

We don't have sex often. Once every three to four weeks. Sometimes even less. At first it really concerned me because I've always been sexual, sensual. I always loved sex.

When we married we were in our early forties. We'd both been married before. We were sexually involved in the seventies—free love and all that.

When we talk about the lack of sex in our marriage, it's with a lot of humor. We think maybe we're fucked out from our youth and reckless years of wildness and craziness when multiple partners weren't dangerous and drugs were a big part of our culture.

But for a while I was really concerned about it. Was I doing it less because I was older—losing my libido? Was it because my husband's not all over me, humping me like a dog? Was it because . . . could it be possible . . . I just don't care about it?

Truly, I think I really don't care—it's such an effort. I'd much rather put this energy elsewhere.

We love each other. We hug and kiss and hold hands. We hang out together. Most of the time we even like each other. It's not unusual for us to be sitting in the living room—he lying on the floor, me on the couch—and one of us will say, "Wanna have sex?" And the other will respond, "Oh yeah, sure, okay." Neither of us will move. We go on with what we're doing. Ten minutes later one of us will ask, "How was it?" and we'll laugh.

The quality of our sex is extraordinary. The quantity—not so. But isn't this part of getting older? Learning quality is better than quantity?

I think sex used to be a tool, a manipulation for me when I was young. A way to get boys, men, hooked on me. It was a performance. With my husband it's love. It's comfortable. It's wonderful to be whatever I am and be unconditionally loved. I'm so lucky to have a partner who's willing to talk and work at our relationship—when it needs work.

It's taken me quite a while—nearly two years—to resolve this issue for myself. My husband's not, nor has he been, as concerned about our lack of sex.

What's helped me some is talking with friends, talking with him. Perhaps I'm more secure in our relationship and with myself.

Everything evolves. Everything becomes clearer as I

move into my mid-forties. Sometimes I'm just amazed I lived through those tumultuous years.

Sandy

"Our passion gives us a privateness in our relationship"

Dear Reader,

It seems that my feelings and ideas about marriage are a function of where I am emotionally, psychologically, financially. Although I thought I had loved, and in a way did love, my first husband, the quality and nature of our love was substantially different from the love I feel now, in my middle years. The predominant recollection I have about my first marriage is that it was a comfortable, safe, and, I thought upon entering it, loving backdrop against which I planned to live out the other aspects of my life.

I always had certain prerequisites for the man I would marry. My choice for my first marriage met these criteria. At the time I was naive and had little, if any, experience as a single woman. I went from my father's house into the arms of a protective college environment and from there directly into a marriage home. In retrospect I can see we were two innocents who were mismatched. We had different expectations and needs and, unfortunately, never had the opportunity to resolve or even discuss or work them out.

I wish I could claim credit for a brilliant choice of husband this time around, but the truth is that he is a random gift from God. I think second marriages can be storybook situations. The first time, because I was younger, it was easy to drift away from the focus of the marriage. With maturity, financial stability, and grown children, it's possible for me, with will and discipline, to tend the relationship. Despite the complications we experience with blending our families, this marriage is more manageable, under most circumstances, than my first marriage, with its tugs and pulls.

There is another element: my husband and I share a high degree of physical passion, and our need and desire, along with the pleasure we gain from physical contact, affirm that our lust is alive and well. This was totally absent from my side of the equation in my first marriage. People have different opinions about the importance of physical connection in relation to a joyful union. Now I can compare my more passive first experience with the true visceral connection we share in this marriage.

Our passion gives us intimacy, a privateness in our relationship. This bond is for the two of us, and only the two of us, and I don't think it can come from anywhere else. So much results from our intimate connection, such as respect and my desire to give pleasure to my husband emotionally as well as physically. I do for him because the pleasure I get in providing for him is my payback.

Barb

"We were like total strangers, still awkward"

Dear Reader,

At the time I couldn't really describe what was wrong. So many things passed through my mind. Occasionally a friend would mention that she and her husband had to get away for a weekend alone. I would feel sad. We could have gotten away but we didn't. My husband and I would make love, but we were like total strangers, still awkward after fourteen years. I wasn't comfortable being sexual with him and I didn't know how to express what was bothering me. Occasionally I would try to talk to him about my feelings or about sex. He'd ignore me or be annoyed. I needed to connect, to feel we were on the same team. He was a brilliant physician. I admired him so much. If he said I was wrong, then he was right. The longer it went on, the more uncomfortable I became. I'd try to tiptoe into the room, adjust my voice, my phrasing. I don't think he approved of me. I couldn't be myself with him.

I was playing tennis one summer. After one of the games, I overheard two women discussing the romantic dinners they were planning for their husbands. The children went away, the sexy underwear came out. Our children had been name tagged, packed, and bussed to camp for a summer of fun too. I came home determined to plan and execute my own romantic evening. I immediately put a bottle of wine in the refrigerator.

What I fantasized wasn't complicated. He'd come home to some wine and cheese. I'd look ravishing. Perfect. I believed I had the key to the locked door.

He came home. We exchanged our usual kiss hello. He didn't notice me or the way my shirt fell against my breast. He didn't notice the cheese and crackers, wine, glasses. All he said was, "Get dressed, we'll go out for dinner." I heard myself explaining how nice it would be to have wine, cheese, and crackers in bed, make love, relax, go for dinner later. He got stuck on the crackers in bed deal, crumbs everywhere, dirt, bugs. I finally convinced him to come upstairs just to make love. Then we got dressed and went out for dinner.

I was in my mid-thirties, a pretty woman who was coming into my own, maybe reaching my sexual peak. Who knows? I didn't have much insight, but something was missing from my marriage.

Stella

"The table looks great. The kitchen is a disaster zone"

Dear Reader,

It had been a long day. One of those days in which appointments seemed to overlap with one another, blending together until I was no longer certain to whom I had said what. The lunch hour had come and gone without my noticing, and now, as I arrived home, my stomach was talking loudly. Dinner would be well appreciated tonight.

We recently remodeled our kitchen and the outlet for the new stovetop exhaust fan is next to the driveway. As I drove toward the garage in back, the aroma of the evening meal wafted through my open window. My wife is a culinary wizard and, even after five years of marriage, the variety of dishes she whips up for a single meal still boggles my mind.

However, my eyes widened and my jaw dropped when I entered the kitchen. Dr. Seuss himself couldn't have imagined a more bizarre sight. Suzanne is a speed cook. There's no better description. She throws together a mouthwatering four-course meal in less than twenty minutes. Tonight, as usual, the table looks great. But the kitchen is a disaster zone. A vast array of pots and pans of all sizes are soaking in a sink full of cold, greasy water. All measuring cups and spoons have been taken from their usual hiding places and strewn along the counter. Never mind only two were required—they were all pulled down. A fine dusting of flour covers the entire kitchen, and the cooktop and much of the counter glisten with a film of splattered grease. The can opener has drippings on it and all of the countertop machines—mixer, toaster, coffee maker, and so on—are coated with the same flour and grease. The uplifting effects of the marvelous aroma quickly fade as I feel depression setting in. Suzanne has outdone herself this evening. Our underlying marital agreement, which keeps our lives running smoothly (relatively speaking), is that each of us capitalizes on our strengths and, in turn, helps compensate for the other's weaknesses. Hence, Suzanne cooks (compensating for the absence of a skill I should have developed more fully during my bachelor days) and I . . . well, I clean.

Opposites attract, or so I've heard. But, once attracted, can they really survive their differences? I'm a very clean cook. Yet my meals are as unimaginative as the kitchen is clean when I'm finished. I try to show Suzanne how to cook with less mess. It doesn't sink in. She, in turn, tries to speed me up (I cook like a mother turtle). Also to no avail. We're not going to change each other's ingrained means of operation. Not that we won't continue to try, with a faint glimmering hope that someday I'll move faster and she'll clean as she cooks. But for now . . .

She looks up with an apologetic smile. "I'll help," she offers.

"What's for supper? Sure smells good," I reply.

Donald

"We both must be right at all times"

Dear Reader,

As I sit ruminating about my marriage, the question that keeps popping up is, Why am I still part of it? We're engaged in a serious struggle for respect and power. I don't quite know when the battle began—probably when I was about four and my father began telling me to be my own boss. I've always taken him quite literally. Unfortunately, someone in Mr. Wonderful's past must have told him the same thing.

So there you have the problem. Two intelligent, stubborn people trying to gain control of each other. If we haven't succeeded in twenty-five years, will we ever? Should we? Discussions in our home usually start at the loud level and go from there. This is because we both must be right at all times.

A few years ago the structure of our marriage changed. I began working and no longer need to depend on my husband for financial support. I could be on my own at any time, and he knows it. Even though he'd die before admitting this, he feels threatened. He has less control, and since I'm not looking for approval, I don't worry about expressing my opinion.

Okay, you say. Something must make me stay in this Golden Gloves of a marriage.

Basically we trust each other. No matter how many times I threaten to leave, I never do, and he never threatens to. I look around at other couples, who seem to have perfect marriages, and one by one they drop by the wayside. One or the other spouse finds out someone is cheating, and they move on. These are often the people who never argue and always treat each other with the utmost respect.

I often wonder how this bickering has affected our kids. Outwardly it hasn't seemed to. They're successful and, although they fight, they seem to share a strong sibling bond. They're not close geographically but they stay in close touch with each other and with us. Although they don't hesitate to express their opinions, they're not particularly argumentative.

So why am I still in the ring? I guess I keep trying to gain the respect I feel I deserve. The loyalty, love, and companionship underlying this union are worth the struggle.

However, we do need to be more courteous to each other. This will keep me in the marriage for another twenty-five-plus years. They say you get testy as you get older. God help us when we're eighty!

Bonnie

"As we get older we cocoon even more"

Dear Reader,

My husband and I accept and love each other the way we are. We have really come to an understanding of how individual we are, and sharing so much brings us together. It is sort of us against the world and as we get older we cocoon even more—we pull a protective shell around ourselves. Although perhaps not consciously, we work on our marriage all the time.

We also share a sense of humor. At the worst moments in our lives, somehow one or the other of us has been able to crack a joke. My mother always said,

"Someday you're going to laugh about this." Maybe there are one or two things we do not laugh about, but there is still time, so we may get to laugh about them yet.

Love underlies our whole relationship. I fell in love with Martin and I have to believe he fell in love with me. When we first met it was almost immediate. Even today, if he is across the room somewhere and I look over and see him talking, the feeling I have after all these years says "love." This is my guy. He is my special person. It is just great. It is chemistry, biology, magic. I wish this for everybody. This spark has to be there and has to stay. There are highs and lows, but this spark makes it all work.

Lanie

"I am able to give in and let go of being right"

Dear Reader,

After graduating from law school, I arranged to move to San Francisco with a guy I had met in D.C. three weeks earlier. He decided to go to law school in San Francisco because I wanted to live there. First I went home to visit my parents.

While I was there, an old flame from San Francisco

came to see me. We fell madly in love again and made plans for him to come live with me on the East Coast. I canceled my California trip and waited for him to return. In the meantime, I met Sam.

We met in a bar and a few days later were in love. We did everything wrong. I was obviously hopping from one relationship to the next. Sam was completely uncool during our courtship. I would be sitting on my back porch with a friend and he would come running up the steps and ask me if this is really still happening. He told me he loved me after we'd known each other for three days. He made it clear he was not going to play hard to get. He introduced me to his friends as "the woman of my dreams."

It was a hot summer and we spent our nights wandering around the city, walking to the park to cool our feet in the fountain. We could not make it down an entire street without stopping to kiss—people were embarrassed by us. We started to live together immediately.

In short, everything looked like it was doomed for failure. This appeared to be like all the other relationships—intense, romantic, and impractical. But I knew this was it because every part of my being told me so. There was never a doubt in my mind. I never found myself looking over at him and wondering what the hell I was doing. Everything felt completely wonderful and right.

I do not think this had anything to do with being

ready for a relationship. (Whenever we had a relationship fail, my women friends and I would say it was because we were not ready.) This had nothing to do with how many hours of therapy I had. There was nothing logical or rational about this. This was love.

My sociology professor taught his students that marriage is meant to be a practical arrangement. A division of labor. The romanticization of marriage in our culture is what leads to disappointment and divorce, he said. My mother, on the other hand, always said that when she married my father there was no doubt in her mind. She was totally in love. To this day she gets weak in the knees when he walks into a room. I believe my mother was right. (My sociology professor ended up divorcing his wife.)

So here I am, five years later. We have been married three years and we have an incredibly adorable and joyful twenty-month-old son. It is true, of course, that we are no longer staring dreamily into each other's eyes and stopping at every park bench to make out. We are working, raising our son, and trying to clean the house once in a while. There are days when we forget to touch each other.

We fight—sometimes big screaming-and-crying-type fights (although that happens less and less). But because there is never a question about whether we will stay together, I feel safe enough to move beyond an adversarial posture (not easy for a lawyer). I am able to give in and let

217

go of being right. In other words, I am able to move beyond the realm of my insecure ego. This is true love.

I never forgot what my mother told me. I could never commit to a relationship when there were doubts. I needed to be absolutely in love from head to toe. I feel the same way to this day. I respect him, I am attracted to him, we have fun together, we dance together, and I absolutely feel we belong together.

Leslie

"I would not change a thing"

Dear one,

> *Ebony eyes from the mine on the knoll*
> *Chestnut hair from the deep*
> *Sinewy, sensitive hands are his prize . . .*
> *Holding my world so complete.*
> *The scar on his face*
> *The jag on his jaw. . . .*

These lines were written thirty-six years ago as part of an ode to you, my then lover, now my husband of thirty-five years. I remember how hard it was for me to breathe when we met.

I could hardly believe you wanted me—country girl

from New Hampshire—you, Bronx Bomber from Morris Avenue. Opposites sure do attract. We were as different as night and day. I was a redheaded WASP and you a smoldering dark-haired Jew. I knew the land, the forest, and the lakes. You knew the bright lights, cement, and rooftops. We both knew French-fried potatoes and Coke. That was about it for similarities. We fell in love. Parents on both sides were probably not happy. We could not have cared less. We were married by the county clerk in Manhattan. My parents grew to love you. Yours never quite made it, I suspect.

We made a major decision early on in our marriage: we opted for a childless future. (We are still glad about that.) So a unique togetherness developed.

As we have aged, so have we seasoned and matured. We have had many ups and only a few downs. I credit you with this fact. You are much easier than I.

As life moves along its ever-rapid track and those around us begin to wrinkle and gray, we marvel at the pace of the years. I know that before long, we too will worry, like those before us, about nurses and canes.

The bodies we inhabit are sure to betray us as we leap for the Retin-A and minute surgical interventions. We laugh heartily about this now. We are convinced of the other's beauty. I still tell you that you were the handsomest man at the party and you, poor-eyed soul, still truly see me as your slim knockout. We are now much more alike than different. Both heads are graying. We live in the city and the country. We cannot find a religious difference and you can chop trees with the best of them but maybe not so swiftly.

If the truth were known, we have almost given up French fries and Cokes for pasta and salad.

Our darling dogs have come and gone—Vivian, Boinky, and Iris. James and Lizzie, named after my grandparents, are in residence now. James is nearly fifteen. We wonder how we will cope with his loss. We focus on him, carefully staying far away from our own artfully concealed mortality. We have taken up golf.

I breathe easily when you enter the room. I wish I did not. I wish we had it to do all over again. I would not change a thing. Would you?

Emily

"Your mother never washed her own back"

Dear Reader,

Ann was my friend in grade school, Brownies, high school, the neighborhood. It was years since I had seen a lot of her, but recently we got together with some of the other girls with whom we grew up.

Over lunch it was Ann's turn to reminisce. To me Ann said, "I always loved to go to your house. Even when we had grown up, your parents were such favorites. I remember one visit. Sometime in the evening your daddy said, 'You'll have to excuse me. I want to turn on the water for Carolyn's bath.'

"A little later, he excused himself again. 'Let me go be sure the water isn't too hot.'"

Then, more dreamily, Ann said, "I always wished that in my life there would be someone who would draw my bath, then check to be sure the temperature was right!"

Mother died four years ago. I visit every morning with my daddy, and every morning wish I had something interesting or funny to bring to our discussions. I couldn't wait to tell him Ann's memories of him.

I told him Ann remembered that he drew Mother's bath and took care that it was as she liked it. Daddy, smiling but deadly earnest, said, "I'm surprised she didn't remember I must have excused myself a third time to wash your mother's back. In the fifty-eight years we were married, except when I was out of town, your mother never washed her own back!"

In truth, I hadn't remembered that he turned on the water or that he checked to see if it was just right. I do remember he always washed her back.

Trudy

Note: *The contributors of this and the next letter are wife and husband.*

"We try never to go to sleep angry"

Dear Reader,

Fifty years of marriage—where have the years gone? However, two children and nine grandchildren and an almost-great-grandchild later, I can see where they've gone. When our parents were married for fifty years, they seemed so old. Why do I still feel young?

We were married during the big war, a four-day honeymoon and then separation for two years. Even though Dave and I went to high school together, we didn't really know each other. We exchanged ideas about what we wanted to do with our lives together through the letters we wrote while we were apart.

After the war, times were hard financially. A daughter was born after two years, followed by a son three years later. My parents died when I was young and we lived with my in-laws for a while. Theirs was the most beautiful marriage and a perfect model for us. They never exchanged a sharp word with each other—not in front of us, anyway.

Our lives have been filled with love for each other

and for our children. We've tried by example to instill in them respect for each other, service to the community, and the necessity of charity. We both worked hard, and now, in our golden years, we're retired and enjoying the fruits of our labor. We try never to go to sleep angry with each other and always to say, "I love you."

Mira

"We hug each other often"

Dear Reader,

My wife sent a separate note. I read it and concur one hundred percent. I really believe we've had a fabulous fifty years of wedded bliss. Some downs (minor ones) but by far mostly ups. We have the deepest respect for each other and, to my knowledge, have never, ever lied, deceived, or tried to cover up anything from each other.

We struggled through some lean years, not having any substantial finances behind us, but we loved playing house with our great family. Our two children are precious to us, different in so many ways that people wonder if they came from the same womb. But we love them equally.

My having a small business that I conducted from our home gave us the unusual opportunity to see a lot of each other, something not too many couples can enjoy. For us, with our similar likes and dislikes, it gave us the opportunity to discuss anything and everything—minor details that came to mind, we discussed right then and there. It really wasn't too much togetherness. On the contrary, it worked out great. When I retired finally, not long ago, we were so used to my being around that it was natural to spend time together without getting in each other's way. It was a mere continuation of a wonderful relationship.

So as a husband who's proud of his fifty years of marriage and hopes for many more, I believe that what contributes to our success is that we always talk out minor problems and differences that arise between us before they fester and get bigger. We hug each other often. It's good for our souls. We're considerate of each other and give in once in a while, even when giving in isn't what we'd like to do.

Dave

"The shell that made me impervious became porous"

Dear Reader,

I have been married a long time—forty-six years. And I have been married all this time to the same woman. Is this an accomplishment? Am I an authority on marriage? I think not. What I am an authority on is my marriage. Even so, I doubt I am aware of all the elements in our relationship, of the changes we have undergone, of the compromises we have made, and of our achievements as a married couple. It may seem strange to use the word "achievement." However, marriage is a relationship that can foster and facilitate growth in a number of areas—personal development, familial development, the development of a home. This is what I have in mind when I refer to the achievements of marriage.

Love is an important aspect of marriage, but it ordinarily is not an achievement except in arranged marriages or marriages of convenience or financial gain. Love usually is, and certainly was for me, a condition for marriage. I won't try to define love. I know I was in love with my wife and she was in love with me. We still are in love with each other, although the form has changed. When we first fell in love, I had a difficult time restraining myself from kissing and fondling her whenever we were together, and we always wanted to be together. Indeed, that's why I married her—so we always could be together. These days the impulse to kiss and fondle her is more restrainable, but it's still there. I suppose someone might say that it was not love in those early days, it was sexual attraction. There was a strong element of sexual attraction in our relationship. However, I have been sexually attracted to women without being in love with them.

We had a lot going for us when we got married. We shared a great many interests—some major, some minor, and all contributing to compatibility. We were both deeply interested in the same professional area. We enjoyed travel and sports. We both loved the theater and had similar reactions to movies, with my wife leaning a bit more to the refined and interpersonally sensitive and I leaning more to the shoot-'em-ups. Despite this bit of sex-typing, our tastes were (and remain) more often similar than different. Of course, we loved children and wanted to have a family.

A related compatibility that was not a factor in our courtship but was a positive factor in the marriage was my wife's interest and skill in cooking and my zest and delight in eating the meals she prepared. I had no idea my bride-to-be was such a wonderful cook. Today we both enjoy dining in fine restaurants, another factor undoubtedly contributing to the longevity of our marriage (although probably not to our individual longevities). However, this was not an initial element in our courtship, since we could not afford fine restaurants. In addition, although I was aware of her beauty, intelligence, and sensitivity, I had little idea of (and, at the time, probably would not have been able to appreciate) the aesthetic sensibilities she would show in decorating our home and looking attractive in inexpensive clothes (all we could afford during the first ten years).

We also began our marriage with some impediments. Our respective families, although loving, were largely sources of problems rather than sources of support. A more fundamental difficulty was our youth and immaturity. I was unable to acknowledge that needs were not being satisfied because we lacked financial resources and my spouse was reluctant to express even modest wants. My view of life required behaving as a good soldier to overcome barriers and frustrations. This, coupled with my self-righteousness, defeated communication and led to spats, emotional outbursts, and a broken record of negative interactions played out in a variety of settings. We sought marriage counseling and individual therapy and finally separated after almost thirty years of marriage. My wife initiated the separation. She took a particularly courageous step in leaving the house, in view of her attachment to home and discomfort with social isolation.

The separation was a shock for me and for her and led to personal growth experiences for both of us. She became more conscious of her needs and better able to effectively articulate them. The impregnable steel shell that made me impervious to some messages, while not shattered, became at least porous. We reconciled after six months.

It took hard work and pain to break down barriers, deepen our understanding of each other, accept our respective failings, and broaden our consciousness. This personal development constitutes for me an important achievement of our marriage. One of the challenges of marriage is for spouses to develop a shared commitment and orientation without sacrificing each other's individuality. Also, for a marriage to work, one partner cannot grow while the other remains suspended in a never-changing time warp of habits and biases.

The creation of a caring, interconnected family is another achievement of our marriage. We are fortunate in having thoughtful and accomplished children who are each creating their own families. A third achievement is a home we enjoy and that serves as a sanctuary and place of support as well as a place for entertaining family and friends. A fourth achievement is a network of friends whom we both care for and enjoy.

I think our marriage illustrates in many ways the gratifications afforded and dilemmas posed by the institution of marriage in our contemporary society. The betrothed are typically two individuals who have only superficial knowledge of each other (although they may believe otherwise) and who, while relatively young, make a lifetime commitment to share a home, raise a family, and remain together. They will have little control over most of the pressures, demands, and problems that life experiences inevitably pose.

In addition to coping with unpredictable events in the external world, the spouses need to adjust to each other's idiosyncrasies as they interact daily and as they change. Hopefully the partners will further develop, deepen, and expand their interests and sensibilities.

The marriage that allows for the gratification and support provided by sharing *plus* personal growth and development for each partner is the marriage we should all strive for. Reaching that goal takes constant work. And work on the part of the marital partners is what is required to make a marriage truly work.

Jake

"Here we are, wrinkles, bellies, and all, laughing more than ever"

Dear Reader,

We take our usual walk this morning, although when I wake up I don't want to move. The dry desert winds stir up my allergies and I feel listless, out of sorts. Staring at my red-rimmed eyes and dry, grooved face as I brush my teeth doesn't help the mood. My hair, standing on end, refuses to be brushed into obedience.

Worse, my knees hurt. I feel like the Tin Woodman in *The Wizard of Oz*, who needed a shot of lubricating oil to get going. The connection of knees—father in wheelchair flashes unhappily in my mind. This was how he lost his independence. He couldn't rely on his knees to walk or drive safely.

"I'm not my father," I say to myself firmly. And more softly, tears just back of my eyes, "Oh, how I miss you, Dad."

"Let's go, darling!" my husband's bright, cheery voice booms from the other room. He speaks loudly, to be heard over the morning news program. I want to go back to bed in silence.

Pete never takes silence for an answer. Knowing me well, he appears in the bedroom doorway to see if I'm dressed and over my rebellion. He resembles an overgrown boy in his turquoise whale sweatshirt (how could I ever have bought it?), bright red pants, mismatched socks, and run-down running shoes. "You'll feel much better once you get going," he says and kisses me.

His kisses always work magic, even when they're illogically timed.

"Okay," I mumble, giving in quickly, knowing he's right.

At our front door we turn left into the ocean breeze, lured by a view of the sea at the end of the street. We pass some teenagers hurrying to get to school in time for their first classes. Pete stops suddenly, grabs my hands, and kisses me. We both giggle. I imagine that any student who sees us thinks we're absurd—two antique creatures in baggy sweats in an embrace.

I feel lucky and blessed and embarrassed, all at once, ready to walk the earth with this man who rarely fails to delight me. Ready to do anything not to have my body go out on me, like the old woman we saw yesterday, frail and dried as an old leaf, clinging to a building for support, stopping for rest before she went on. He's right. I need the exercise to get my mental and physical kinks out.

We walk to the park bordering the beach, lost in our own thoughts. "See you at Willow Street," he says and begins to jog slowly, still-muscular legs as sturdy as ever, belly an unwelcome, perhaps permanent, visitor.

All the things I wanted to change in him now seem curiously appealing—his passion for golf, his sloppy habits, and his invariable optimism. Golf gives him exercise, friendship, and fresh air and helps him slug back at business frustration, and I'd rather pick up after him than have him be a nitpicker, railing at me for being sporadically messy. I know he'll never change. I don't want him to anymore. We are what we are, and somehow my occa-

231

sional pessimism and his optimism are the perfect dancers, bridging the changing rhythms of life. And he's more thoughtful than ever, in all the important ways.

Where did all the years go? Gone, leaving us photographs on the family wall and a residue of the silver stardust that is love.

We meet again at Willow, our favorite street. "Do you still want a home here?" he asks, as though we aren't backed to the wall financially, as though we aren't in debt, as though the recession never happened.

"No," I answer, as if the choice is real. "I don't want a house anymore. I feel more secure in our condo because I'm not afraid to be alone when you're out of town. It's just right for the two of us."

"We could get a dog again," he smiles. "A big Saint Bernard, just like Reggie." I think of the rainy night in 1979, when I could no longer deny that our marriage was in deep trouble. We were lying on the den floor in our tract home, Reggie happily curled between us. A soft-porn movie came on and he petted the dog languidly, never thinking of reaching out for me. I remember the ache of being unwanted, of getting up silently and going to bed without washing my face, pretending I was asleep when he came in. When I'm upset, I don't pretend anymore. I talk about it. I don't have the patience to wait. I've learned that much. The more honest I am, the less seems to come up.

The street slopes imperceptibly uphill, but my lungs want more air than I can take in and I fall behind his brisk pace. He turns, missing me.

"I'm not too speedy this morning," I pant. "Go ahead. I'll catch up."

"No. I don't ever want to leave you behind," he says and slows to take my hand and kiss me tenderly.

Memory wants to accuse him: "But you did leave me! You did! Don't you remember? Can you block out everything?" Why can't I do this? It would make life so much easier.

I stop the downward spiral of the blame game. That stage is over. I have nothing to worry about now but time. We're here for each other in a way we never were before, when we glossed over our differences to preserve the image of the perfect marriage. Here we are, wrinkles, bellies, and all, laughing more than ever at the foibles we no longer try to change.

I reach up like a young bride to touch his face, the curve of his cheek, and tilt my face to kiss him. I think I'd rather be here, right now, right this moment, feeling this way, than be young again with perfect knees. I laugh at the unspoken joy that bubbles up, and he looks at me and says appreciatively, "Does any couple laugh as much as we do?" He slides his right hand under the band of my sweatpants, grabbing my behind, knowing I never wear underpants on our walks for exactly this moment.

"No couple I know," I respond. "My behind is getting so much smaller!" We both laugh again at my forty-year battle with a flabby butt.

"I can hardly find it," he says, so sincere I almost believe him.

We walk on, a little slower now. His thoughts, I can tell, are on business.

Mine linger on children, grandchildren, and marriage. How many marriages are stronger after a separation? Ours is. Eleven years ago we parted, at his request. He had fallen in love with a younger woman, an employee. We were apart for a year and a half, and I thought I'd never recover from the pain and the anger and the loss of him, but I did. I learned to appreciate myself when I didn't have him to please. Best lesson I ever learned.

So it has come to this: Noticing thoughts fly through my mind like a flock of birds. I choose this one and that, not feeling their prisoner—most of the time. Noticing we're in the fall of our lives, amazed that spring and summer have gone . . . wondering when winter will come.

Charlotte

Afterword

Working with the letters heightened our awareness, especially of our spouses' points of view. The letters drew our attention to factors that are common to marriages and that nourish or deplete them.

Looking at these marriages, we have a new understanding of what commitment means. Now we think of the joining together that characterizes commitment as rooted in the respect, understanding, patience, and caring we show our spouses. We are reminded of how much attention goes into making a satisfying marriage.

The writers, as a group, have endured many challenges—illnesses, wars, separations, the repercussions of past events—and frequently attribute the strength of their marriages to having survived these adversities together.

Marriages constantly change, and, as individuals, so

do wives and husbands. The contributors vary widely in their feelings about change and change resonates through the letters—what happens when spouses try to change each other or themselves, how couples change in response to crises and illness, changes that result when spouses become parents or remarry, and why change is essential.

A number of the writers refer to marriage as a journey. We like to travel, so this metaphor appeals to us. Travel, of course, like marriage, enables us to understand our lives differently. Through the letters, we have come to know our traveling companions and, as well, become more knowledgeable about ourselves. These letters give us the comfort of knowing we are in good company.

*A*cknowledgments

First, we express our gratitude to the contributors who allowed us into their lives, and whose participation made this book possible. We thank them for the thought and effort they put into their letters, and for their confidence in us. We thank everyone who wrote, although, regrettably, we were not able to include every letter.

Our thanks go also to Lois Herzeca, dear friend, lawyer, and enthusiastic supporter, for reading and commenting on all the drafts; Judith Fein, Ellen Woliner, Todd Rhoda, Sarah Milroy, Carol Snow, and Susan Evans for sharing their expertise; Sandra Fowler, Barbara Ramalho, and Deirdre Clarke for helping in so many ways; Peter Freeman and Jeff Spielberg, for demystifying computers; Malcolm J. Rothbard, M.D., for making a special introduction; Norma Feshbach, Ph.D., professor and friend, for providing us with our first opportunity to collaborate; and Judith Riven, our agent who has become our friend, for understanding what we wanted to do and helping us make it happen. We particularly want to thank Cynthia Vartan, our editor, for her guidance and humor, and Wendy Sherman and everyone at Henry Holt and Company for their support.

To all our friends for their love and patience during the times when we had no time, and to one friend whose experiences inadvertently set this book in motion. To our sisters, Daryl Roth and Ann Powell.

To our families, whose understanding and support made it possible for us to give this book the attention it deserved.

About the Editors

DALE ATKINS, PH.D., is a psychologist, educator, and lecturer. She is a nationally recognized expert and consultant in the field of family communication and is a frequent guest on national television and radio shows. She is the author of *Sisters* as well as many articles and professional publications. Dr. Atkins has a private practice in New York City and lives in Connecticut with her husband and two sons.

MERIS POWELL, M.A., is a writer and editor whose graduate degree is in developmental and educational psychology. She is also a fund-raiser and advocate for children and families. Ms. Powell is experienced in television development, production, and marketing, and has been working on a biography for television. She lives in New York City with her husband and daughter.